# John Mark
## The author of the first Gospel

# John Mark
## The author of the first Gospel

*A school of thought on his
world, his family, the people
that surrounded him, and the
principal influences in his life*

Prince Maurice Parker, Th.D.
Assemblies of God Theological Seminary
La Carlota, Córdoba
Spain

XULON PRESS

Xulon Press
2301 Lucien Way #415
Maitland, FL 32751
407.339.4217
www.xulonpress.com

© 2019 by Prince Maurice Parker, Th.D.

All rights reserved solely by the author. The author guarantees all contents are original and do not infringe upon the legal rights of any other person or work. No part of this book may be reproduced in any form without the permission of the author. The views expressed in this book are not necessarily those of the publisher.

Unless otherwise indicated, Scripture quotations taken from (Version(s) used:

**1599 Geneva Bible** (GNV) Geneva Bible, 1599 Edition. Published by Tolle Lege Press. All rights reserved. No part of this publication may be reproduced or transmitted in any form or by any means, electronic or mechanical, without written permission from the publisher, except in the case of brief quotations in articles, reviews, and broadcasts.

**21st Century King James Version** (KJ21) Copyright © 1994 by Deuel Enterprises, Inc.

**American Standard Version** (ASV) Public Domain

**Amplified Bible** (AMP) Copyright © 2015 by The Lockman Foundation, La Habra, CA 90631. All rights reserved.

**Amplified Bible, Classic Edition** (AMPC) Copyright © 1954, 1958, 1962, 1964, 1965, 1987 by The Lockman Foundation.

**BRG Bible** (BRG) Blue Red and Gold Letter Edition™ Copyright © 2012 BRG Bible Ministries. Used by Permission. All rights reserved. BRG Bible is a Registered Trademark in U.S. Patent and Trademark Office #4145648

**Christian Standard Bible** (CSB) Copyright © 2017 by Holman Bible Publishers. Used by permission. Christian Standard Bible®, and CSB® are federally registered trademarks of Holman Bible Publishers, all rights reserved.

**Common English Bible** (CEB) Copyright © 2011 by Common English Bible.

**Complete Jewish Bible** (CJB) Copyright © 1998 by David H. Stern. All rights reserved.

**Contemporary English Version** (CEV) Copyright © 1995 by American Bible Society

**Darby Translation** (DARBY) Public Domain

**Disciples' Literal New Testament** (DLNT) Disciples' Literal New Testament: Serving Modern Disciples by More Fully Reflecting the Writing Style of the Ancient Disciples, Copyright © 2011 Michael J. Magill. All Rights Reserved. Published by Reyma Publishing.

**Douay-Rheims 1899 American Edition** (DRA) Public Domain

**Douay-Rheims Bible** (DRB) © Copyright DRBO.org 2001-2019. All Rights Reserved.

**Easy-to-Read Version** (ERV) Copyright © 2006 by Bible League International

**Evangelical Heritage Version** (EHV) The Evangelical Heritage Version (EHV), New Testament & Psalms ©2017

**English Majority Text Version** (EMTV) Copyright © 2009 By Paul W. Esposito.

**English Standard Version** (ESV) The Holy Bible, English Standard Version. ESV® Text Edition: 2016. Copyright © 2001 by Crossway Bibles, a publishing ministry of Good News Publishers.

**English Standard Version Anglicised** (ESVUK) The Holy Bible, English Standard Version Copyright © 2001 by Crossway Bibles, a division of Good News Publishers.

**Expanded Bible** (EXB) The Expanded Bible, Copyright © 2011 Thomas Nelson Inc. All rights reserved.

**GOD'S WORD** Translation (GW) Copyright © 1995 by God's Word to the Nations. Used by permission of Baker Publishing Group

**Greek Old Testament** (Greek OT), Deutsche Bibelgesellschaft, Balinger Straße 31A 70567 Stuttgart Germany. Revised ed. edition (9 Mar. 2007).

**Holman Christian Standard Bible** (HCSB) Copyright © 1999, 2000, 2002, 2003, 2009 by Holman Bible Publishers, Nashville Tennessee. All rights reserved.

**International Children's Bible** (ICB) The Holy Bible, International Children's Bible® Copyright© 1986, 1988, 1999, 2015 by Tommy Nelson™, a division of Thomas Nelson. Used by permission.

**International Standard Version** (ISV) Copyright © 1995-2014 by ISV Foundation. ALL RIGHTS RESERVED INTERNATIONALLY. Used by permission of Davidson Press, LLC.

**J.B. Phillips New Testament** (PHILLIPS) The New Testament in Modern English by J.B Phillips copyright © 1960, 1972 J. B. Phillips. Administered by The Archbishops' Council of the Church of England. Used by Permission.

**King James Version** (KJV) Public Domain

**Authorized (King James) Version** (AKJV) KJV reproduced by permission of Cambridge University Press, the Crown's patentee in the UK.

**Lexham English Bible** (LEB) 2012 by Logos Bible Software. Lexham is a registered trademark of Logos Bible Software

**Living Bible** (TLB) The Living Bible copyright © 1971 by Tyndale House Foundation. Used by permission of Tyndale House Publishers Inc., Carol Stream, Illinois 60188. All rights reserved.

**Modern English Version** (MEV) The Holy Bible, Modern English Version. Copyright © 2014 by Military Bible Association. Published and distributed by Charisma House.

**Names of God Bible** (NOG) The Names of God Bible (without notes) © 2011 by Baker Publishing Group.

**New American Bible** (Revised Edition) (NABRE) Scripture texts, prefaces, introductions, footnotes, and cross references used in this work are taken from the New American Bible, revised edition © 2010, 1991, 1986, 1970 Confraternity of Christian Doctrine, Inc., Washington, DC All Rights Reserved. No part of this work may be reproduced or transmitted in any form or by any means, electronic or mechanical, including photocopying, recording, or by any information storage and retrieval system, without permission in writing from the copyright owner.

**New Century Version** (NCV) The Holy Bible, New Century Version®. Copyright © 2005 by Thomas Nelson, Inc.

**New English Translation** (NET) NET Bible® copyright ©1996-2006 by Biblical Studies Press, L.L.C. http://netbible.com All rights reserved.

**New International Reader's Version** (NIRV) Copyright © 1995, 1996, 1998, 2014 by Biblica, Inc.®. Used by permission. All rights reserved worldwide.

**New International Version** (NIV) Holy Bible, New International Version®, NIV® Copyright ©1973, 1978, 1984, 2011 by Biblica, Inc.® Used by permission. All rights reserved worldwide.

**New International Version - UK** (NIVUK) Holy Bible, New International Version® Anglicized, NIV® Copyright © 1979, 1984, 2011 by Biblica, Inc.® Used by permission. All rights reserved worldwide.

**New King James Version** (NKJV) Scripture taken from the New King James Version®. Copyright © 1982 by Thomas Nelson. Used by permission. All rights reserved.

**New Living Translation** (NLT) Holy Bible, New Living Translation, copyright © 1996, 2004, 2015 by Tyndale House Foundation. Used by permission of Tyndale House Publishers, Inc., Carol Stream, Illinois 60188. All rights reserved.

**New Revised Standard Version** (NRSV) New Revised Standard Version Bible, copyright © 1989 the Division of Christian Education of the National Council of the Churches of Christ in the United States of America. Used by permission. All rights reserved.

**New Revised Standard Version, Anglicised** (NRSVA) New Revised Standard Version Bible: Anglicised Edition, copyright © 1989, 1995 the Division of Christian Education of the National Council of the Churches of Christ in the United States of America. Used by permission. All rights reserved.

**New Revised Standard Version, Anglicised Catholic Edition** (NRSVACE) New Revised Standard Version Bible: Anglicised Catholic Edition, copyright © 1989, 1993, 1995 the Division of Christian Education of the National Council of the Churches of Christ in the United States of America. Used by permission. All rights reserved.

**New Revised Standard Version Catholic Edition** (NRSVCE) New Revised Standard Version Bible: Catholic Edition, copyright © 1989, 1993 the Division of Christian Education of the National Council of the Churches of Christ in the United States of America. Used by permission. All rights reserved.

**New Testament for Everyone** (NTE) Scripture quotations from The New Testament for Everyone are copyright © Nicholas Thomas Wright 2011.

**Revised Standard Version** (RSV) Revised Standard Version of the Bible, copyright © 1946, 1952, and 1971 the Division of Christian Education of the National Council of the Churches of Christ in the United States of America. Used by permission. All rights reserved.

**Tree of Life Version** (TLV) Tree of Life (TLV) Translation of the Bible. Copyright © 2015 by The Messianic Jewish Family Bible Society.

**The Voice** (VOICE)The Voice Bible Copyright © 2012 Thomas Nelson, Inc. The Voice™ translation © 2012 Ecclesia Bible Society All rights reserved.

**The Scriptures** (TS2009) Copyright © 1993-2015 by the Institute for Scripture Research (ISR) All Rights Reserved.

**World English Bible** (WEB) by Public Domain. The name "World English Bible" is trademarked.

**Worldwide English** (New Testament) (WE) © 1969, 1971, 1996, 1998 by SOON Educational Publications

**Wycliffe Bible** (WYC) 2001 by Terence P. Noble.

Printed in the United States of America.

ISBN-13: 978-1-54566-956-3

# DEDICATION

To my beloved wife and perfect help meet for me, Guillermina Olmos de Parker (Gina), the manifestation in the flesh of Proverbs 31, and my three daughters: Hilda Guadalupe Parker de Jesús, Genesis Parker-Davis, Myrrh Jasmine Parker-Hampton, and last, but not least my son, Jason Uriel Parker. Thank you!

# I WANT TO THANK:

The rector of our seminary, Dr. Jesús Manuel Caramés Tenreiro, and my colleagues: Dr. Levi De Carvalho, Osmani Cruz Ferrer, y Jesús Javier Gómez Gómez, and Pastor Esteban Muñoz de Morales, highly esteemed professors of the seminary that I have the privilege to know, and that refresh and challenge me continually with the crisp intellects and highly tuned academia. They have helped me with their patience by reading this manuscript and offer their observations and valuable criteria.

# TABLE OF CONTENTS

**Abstract** .................................................. **xv**
**Introduction** ............................................ **xvii**
    *An Unexpected and Historical Invitation* .......... *xviii*
    *The Details of the Masks* ............................ *xxi*

**Chapter 1: What is the Gospel of Mark?** ................ **1**
    *Mark as a foundation* ................................. *2*
    *The Authorship of the Gospel of Mark* ............... *3*
    *Details of the Gospel of Mark* ....................... *5*
    *Simon Peter's Influence* ............................. *6*
    *Historical Clues and Indications* .................. *11*
    *Who was John Mark?* ................................. *12*

**Chapter 2: Influences That Provoke an Eisegesis**
              **and Not an Exegesis** ................... **16**
    *An Exegetical Bridge* ............................... *16*
    *It Was Very Good* ................................... *17*
    *The Beginning of the Departure* ..................... *19*
    *Holiness and the Eucharist* ......................... *21*
    *The Roman Empire and the Roman Catholic Church* .... *23*
    *The Catholic Influence* ............................. *26*
    *Celibacy* ........................................... *28*
    *A Logical and Natural Part of the Perfect Plan of God* ... *31*
    *Moses and The Levites* .............................. *33*
    *Jeremiah and Ezekiel* ............................... *33*
    *Abraham, "Ishmael," Isaac, and Jacob* ............... *34*
    *The Messiah* ........................................ *36*
    *Continuing with the Subject* ........................ *37*

**Chapter 3 – Marriage in the New Testament**..........**38**
   *The Family of the Lord Jesus Christ* .................*38*
   *The Genealogies of Matthew and Luke* ..............*38*
   *Continuing with Christ's Family*.....................*42*
   *James*....................................................*43*
   *James as an Apostol* ..................................*45*
   *Jude* ....................................................*48*

**Chapter 4: Examples of Unrecognized Families** .......**51**
   *The Road to Emmaus*.................................*51*
   *Mary, Mary, Mary* ...................................*52*
   *Diverse Languages*...................................*57*
   *Cleopas y Zebedee*...................................*61*
   *A Fisherman from Galilee with a House the Judea* ....*62*
   *Mara, Mary, Miriam, Maryam, Mirjam* ..............*64*
   *Originally, What Did It Mean to Be a Jew?*...........*65*
   *Ethiopian Jews*.......................................*71*
   *Jews in the Northern Kingdom*......................*75*
   *Now, Back to the "Marys"*...........................*80*
   *Back to the Road to Emmaus* .......................*83*

**Chapter 5: John Mark** ................................**85**
   *The Relationship Between John Mark*
      *and Joseph of Cyprus* ..........................*85*
   *Barnabas; The Leader Maker*.......................*88*

**Chapter 6: John Mark's Mother**......................**97**

**Chapter 7 – The Relationship Between**
      **John Mark and Paul**.....................**104**
   *Background*.........................................*104*
   *Barnabas, Paul, and John Mark*....................*108*

**Chapter 8 - The Relationship Between**
   **Simon Peter and John Mark** ...................**116**
   *What We Know of Simon Peter* .....................*121*
   *A Reality for Peter, and a Hypothetical*
      *Situation for Us* ................................*127*

*I want to Thank:*

    *Mark in Gethsemane* . . . . . . . . . . . . . . . . . . . . . . . . . . . . .*130*
    *Peter's Sudden, but Temporary Dilemma*. . . . . . . . . . .*132*
    *Back to the Garden*. . . . . . . . . . . . . . . . . . . . . . . . . . . . . .*133*
    *Following the Path of Logical Deduction* . . . . . . . . . . . .*134*

**Conclusion** . . . . . . . . . . . . . . . . . . . . . . . . . . . . . . . . . . . . . **137**
**Bibliography** . . . . . . . . . . . . . . . . . . . . . . . . . . . . . . . . . . . **141**
**Online Books and Resources**. . . . . . . . . . . . . . . . . . . . . . **145**
**Bible Translations That Were Employed**
    **in This Work** . . . . . . . . . . . . . . . . . . . . . . . . . . . . . . . . . **147**

# RECOMMENDATION

I have had the pleasure and the honor to know the author of this book, Dr. Prince Parker, and his lovely wife Guillermina, for many years. For decades they have served in the work of the Lord here in Spain in the regions of Castilla La Mancha, Extremadura, and now, in Andalucía. This causes me to feel a profound debt of gratitude and admiration for the faithfulness they have to their call to seek the spiritual well-being of my country with the Gospel of Jesus Christ.

Dr. Prince has always been detailed and meticulous in what he does, and this literary work is no exception. His approach to Mark the evangelist reveals the influences on his life as well as his historical and sociocultural backgrounds. This also challenges us intellectually to discover a multitude of details that bring a new significance to this Gospel. These details help us to find and place the missing pieces that were lacking in our understanding and even change some of the perceptions that we might have previously held.

I recommend this book to all avid and studied readers, to those that are not satisfied with superficial positions and are desirous to dive deeper into the wisdom of God that is revealed in His Word.

Esteban Muñoz de Morales Mohedano<br>
Assistant General Superintentent<br>
Assemblies of God of Spain (FADE)<br>
https://asambleasdedios.es/

---

Pastor<br>
Comunidad de Amor Cristiano (CAC)<br>
Plaza Lahore 1,<br>
C.P. 14007 Córdoba - Spain<br>
http://iglesiacac.es/

Dr. Parker has been able to take us into the depth of this surprising and innovative examination on the life of John Mark the Evangelist. With extraordinary mastery, he turns the reader into an investigator in such a way that you become a participant, not only in the discovery but also the satisfaction of this unique encounter.

Dr. Jesús Manuel Caramés Tenreiro

Rector

Assemblies of God Theological Seminary

(Facultad de Teología)

Assemblies of God of Spain

La Carlota, Córdoba

Spain

# ABSTRACT

I want to present a school of thought concerning the life and family relationships of John Mark. To do this, I will take the time to build a broad foundation over which I will construct my argument. In the formation of this platform, I will develop the various concepts, that, at first, might seem to be unrelated to our theme, but will manifest their value and show themselves to be indispensably relevant to the original context.

Also, in the development of this ideological platform, I will display the historical and sociocultural influences that I believe have provoked an eisegesis of the Scriptures concerning several aspects of our subject matter. These influences have instilled concepts and perceptions that distort our understanding and rob us of the riches found in certain aspects of the beautiful message presented in the autographs by the author.[1] Without these influences and taking a posture and a more practical and holistic approach, we can have a more definite sense of the situations that we see in the New Testament.

Also presented will be particular influences and historical backgrounds that marked specific characteristics of the culture and situations of Judea and the Galilean regions of the first century. This will be done to help us understand that which we

---

[1] In biblical parlance, the autographs refer to the original documents of the books of the Bible in their original languages.

read in the Scriptures. In this process, I will take the time to indicate these features to build a bridge from the first century to our present day.

Consequently, we will be able to see without the interferences of the influences of our present era that have deviated our comprehension of the authentic ambiance and the world of John Mark. Likewise, I will give coherence to the Scriptures to show the stunning picture they paint for us. This process will also show us cases of other Biblical personalities that were related by blood or marriage that we do not commonly associate in such a manner.

Touching John Mark's extrabiblical history, we will investigate the criteria and commentaries of historical figures of the second century and throughout the history of the church, religious entities, and the observations and opinions of selected theologians and historians.

I hope that by presenting this exegetical evidence that affirms that which I explicate and clarify, that we will better understand the Scriptures that will be analyzed.

**Keywords**: Exegetics; Gospels; Sociocultural Perspective; Geopolitical Perspective; Philology, etymology, linguistic Influence; History; Early Church Leaders; Families in the Bible.

## Introduction

# THE BEGINNING

Some might wonder why I would write a commentary on Mark as an example of practical exegesis. Like all honest questions, this is a good one! The answer is that I find that by writing this simple investigation touching the various aspects of the Gospel of Mark that I want to highlight, I can touch, and even go deep into certain historical aspects of just about the entire Bible. I want to investigate, primarily, the customs and sociocultural characteristics of the New Testament world, with a focus on Mark and his world.

Also, by investigating Mark, I touch on every major character of the New Testament. As we will see in more detail, Mark was the first Gospel written, and the other two Synoptics almost certainly used His Gospel as a format for their excellent investigations and testimonies. Mark had direct, or indirect contact and personal knowledge of almost every major character of the New Testament.

Acts 12 shows us that he knew Peter, and extra-biblical historical records also affirm that he knew him exceptionally well. By the confidence that the Apostle Peter had with his house in Acts 12, and the message that was sent to his house to the other apostles (Acts 12:17), we can safely conclude that he knew the other Apostles too. He, undoubtedly, was related to Barnabas and worked side-by-side with the Apostle Paul while Paul was under Barnabas. Later, when Paul was an aged veteran of the apostleship, Mark was counted as one of his trusted co-laborers.

By studying his life, family, physical, geographical surroundings, those with whom he was associated, we can learn an incredible amount of the entire New Testament environment, the other Gospels and even answer questions that can leave people perplexed or with sad misconceptions that are capable of robbing us of the beauty of God's Word.

A few years ago, I did an investigation on the background of the life, and sociocultural environment of Simon Peter. A few years later I wrote a commentary on the Gospel of Mark for use in my church, and in the Bible studies of the churches that I had established. All this did was to provoke me to investigate even deeper into the lives of these two Biblical personalities. From the very beginning, I noticed that the more that I studied, the more that I discovered that they were practically inseparable.

With this study, I want to enter certain aspects of the world in which these two protagonists lived that held such an influence over their lives. I wanted to know the details of the people that surrounded them; people that they knew very well. I also wanted to know how all of this was reflected in their actions and decisions.

## An Unexpected and Historical Invitation

In April of 2015, I was invited to go to Jerusalem in June to witness the introduction, to a limited public, of a great

*The Beginning*

archeological find of fragments of the Gospel of Mark. The presenter of these artifacts was Dr. Craig Evans, professor of the New Testament in *Acadia Divinity College in Wolfville*, Nova Scotia, Canada. He and his team of investigators of around three dozen scientists and assorted academics found the oldest fragments of this Gospel in a find of Egyptian death mask made of papyrus.[2] These fragments could hold the same value for the New Testament that the Dead Sea Scrolls have for the Old Testament.

The reason that this Discovery is so transcendental is that we have fragments of the Gospels from the second century. For example, a portion of the Gospel of John from the years between 101-200 A.D., is in exposition in Sotheby's auction house in London.[3] Nevertheless, the fragments of these mummy masks are considerably older, giving evidence of being from the middle or near the end of the first century; very possibly from around the decade of the 80s A.D.

At the time of this writing, though Dr. Evans' investigative team has not completed the official publication of their discovery, they hold that by way of Carbon-14 analysis, calligraphy, and a comparison of texts, that it can be confirmed that the funeral masks are Egyptian and from the first century.

---

[2] Owen Jarus. *Mummy Mask May Reveal Oldest Known Gospel*, Live Science - History, January 18, 2015 04:21am ET. https://www.livescience.com/49489-oldest-known-gospel-mummy-mask.html. (Accessed el 01/04/2015)

[3] Laura Clark. *Papyrus Found in a Mummy Mask May Be the Oldest Known Copy of a Gospel*, Smithsonian.com, January 21, 2015. https://www.smithsonianmag.com/smart-news/papyrus-found-mummy-mask-may-be-oldest-known-copy-gospel-180953962/ (Accessed el 01/04/2015).

Santiago Guijarro is a professor of the New Testament of the Pontific University in Salamanca, Spain, and director of the Spanish Biblical Association. He is not an official part of Dr. Evans' team, but he too puts the date of these fragments in the first century around the decades of the 80s A.D. If this, is indeed is the case, the evidence that we have sustains the idea that they can be up to one hundred years older than the fragment of Sotheby.

Before this finding, the "Rylands Library Papyrus P52, also known as the St John's fragment", was the oldest known manuscript portion of the New Testament. It is kept in the John Rylands Library located in Manchester, United Kingdom.[4]

This papyrus contains text from the Gospel of John dated around 125-130 A.D. It shows that the last of the four Gospels, that according to the tradition, was written between 90 and 100 A.D. This fragment (that, of course, was once a part of an entire document) was circulating in Egypt within forty years of its composition. It is possible that this papyrus originated in Egypt from where it was acquired in 1917.[5]

Biblical academics and historians agree that even though the epistle of James is the oldest book of the New Testament, the Gospel of Mark is the first and oldest Gospel written. We assert that it was written in the first century during a period in which many of the eyewitnesses of the life, death, and resurrection of the Lord Jesus Christ were still alive.

---

[4] Raymond E. Brown. *El Evangelio según Juan. Vol. I.* Madrid: Ediciones Cristiandad. p. 104. "... ha sido ampliamente aceptada la datación de este papiro en 135-50."

[5] F.F. Bruce. "*The New Testament Documents: Are they Reliable?* North Kingston, RI: Kingsley Books; p. 9. 2018.

Even though this has been our assertion, some critics have wanted to establish later dates for the writing of all the Gospels. Nevertheless, even though we base our affirmation on the testimony of the Scriptures and other historical sources, this is the first time that we can argue with physical evidence at hand.

## The Details of the Masks

The rich and powerful in ancient Egypt were buried with death masks that were made of gold and luxurious artistic handiwork. Those dignitaries of a slightly lesser status might have artifacts of silver; and those following them, adornments of bronze. A lower status even still might have earned them the worthy honor of a mummy mask of wood. However, among the poorest that wished to honor their dead, masks of linens, or papyrus with glue and Paint would be fashioned. They devised ways of making durable papier-mache masks and painted them with the hand that best knew how, and according to what they could afford.

Unfortunately, even papyrus was an expensive substance and challenging to acquire for the impoverished. When we consider that most of the poor were illiterate, what was written on the papyruses that they had found to honor their dead held little to nothing of importance or value to them.

A technique has been developed to separate the sheets of papyrus without damaging them in such a way that we can easily read the text that is written on them. While this was being done, each little step of the entire procedure was being documented. Notwithstanding, those that opposed the Project did so because valuable ancient artifacts were being destroyed in the process.

Undaunted by this opposition, this team of archeologists esteemed that the value of the fragments found was of greater worth than the masks that contained them. This would be comparable to having to break through the rock wall of an ancient chamber to find more significant and more valuable artifacts than the wall that hid the compartment.

Furthermore, the only masks that were destroyed were the ones that were not esteemed apt for museum display. Based on this estimation of worth, the decision was made to go ahead with the investigation to examine and see if something, if anything at all, could be found on the papyruses used in these masks. As a result, they estimated that what they found was of far higher value than the very masks that contained these document fragments.

It was discovered that these masks contained a wealth of, not only the fragments of the Gospel of Mark but of other pieces of ancient literature as well. In an interview with Live Science, Dr. Evans said:

> *We're recovering ancient documents from the first, second and third centuries. Not just Christian documents, not just biblical documents, but classical Greek texts, business papers, various mundane papers, personal letters, ... The documents include philosophical texts and copies of stories by the Greek poet Homer.*

Some of the other documents have dates that help to corroborate the test that they are performing to confirm and establish the ages of the fragments of the Gospel of Mark.

Consequently, I will conclude here by saying that which I have mentioned, that what we have with these fragments is that they are the New Testament equivalent to the value of the Dead Sea Scrolls for the Old Testament.

# Chapter 1

# WHAT IS THE GOSPEL OF MARK?

When you hear this question, you might consider it almost elementary or infantile. It is seemingly evident that it is the ocular testimony of the life of our Lord Jesus Christ.

Nevertheless, if we investigate the background of the Gospel, we can see that this question carries much more weight. It is not possible to determine the precise date in which this Gospel was written. Biblical historians vacillate between the years 55 and 70 A.D. However, I am firmly in agreement with F.F. Bruce when he says:

> *Many modern academics place the dates of the four Gospels in the following manner: Matthew, near 85-90 A.D.; Mark, near 65 A.D.; Luke, near 80-85 A.D.; John, near 90-100 A.D.*
>
> *I am inclined to put the dates of the first three Gospels much earlier: Mark a Little after 60 A.D., Luke between 60 and 70 A.D., and Matthew right after 70 A.D. A criterion that weighs heavily with me is the relation that these writings have with the destruction of the city and the Temple of*

> *Jerusalem by the Romans in 70 A.D. My perspective is that Mark and Luke were written before this event, and Matthew not much afterward.*[6]

## Mark as a Foundation

It is evident that Matthew and Luke did their investigations to compile testimonies for their Gospels. Matthew was an eyewitness of the events and readily had access to interview Mary and other protagonists involved in the life of Christ before he was called to follow Jesus. On the other hand, Luke said that his Gospel was the combination of the compilation of testimonies that were related to him by eyewitnesses that were with Christ from the beginning, as well as his investigations (Luke 1:1-3).

Nevertheless, it is without a doubt that both used the Gospel of Mark as an outline to follow and to write their accounts with far more details and order. We do not have to study the Gospels deeply to see that the three testimonies have much in common, and, for this reason, they are called the Synoptics. Being that we have established that the Gospel of Mark was written before the other two, we can affirm the following: We find that 606 of 661 verses of Mark appear in similar form in Matthew, and 350 of Mark's verses appear in Luke with little or no variations at all.[7]

Now then, we cannot avoid the fact of the fundamental similarity of the testimonies. This resemblance is desired and

---

[6] F.F. Bruce. *The New Testament Documents: Are they Reliable?* North Kingston, RI: Kingsley Books; p. 6. 2018.

[7] William Hendriksen. *New Testament Commentary: Exposition of the Gospel According to Matthew.* Grand Rapids, MI: Baker Book House, 1973.

expected because they are writing of the same factual and historical events in which they were eyewitnesses or are relating interviews of those that witnessed the same events. If you want to establish a legal case, you seek the similitude of testimonies that we see in the Gospels with details and distinctive from the perspectives of the individual onlookers.

However, the similitude of these mentioned verses is evidence that the Gospel of Mark was the mutual document used by Luke and Matthew to write their marvelous testimonies in a more developed and illustrative manner. At times, the material is so identical that one would be hard pressed to consider this an accidental occurrence.

## The Authorship of the Gospel of Mark

The authorship of the Gospels has long been a matter of considerable debate among skeptics and detractors of the Canon of the New Testament. The Gospel of Mark is the account of the life, ministry, death, and resurrection of Jesus Christ. However, as per John Mark, by name, nothing is said directly about him as being a witness in any of the Gospels. How then can we attribute the authorship of this Gospel to him with such a high degree of assurance and confidence? We can also ask from where Mark got his information concerning Jesus.

By reading the Gospel of Luke and the book of Acts we can conclude, by the internal evidence that we find, that the author is indeed Luke. However, we find no such overwhelming evidence that confirms that John Mark is the author of the Gospel that bears his name. Nevertheless, all the writers of the first centuries of the early church unanimously attribute the authorship of the book to John Mark.

For example, the oldest testimony of the authorship of this Gospel is from Papias of Hierapolis and is from around the year 140 A.D.

Papias was the bishop of Hierapolis, in Phrygia, and he refers to this Gospel in his work, "*Exegesis of the oracles of Jesus.*" Portions of this writing were found in fragments of "*Ecclesiastical History*" by Eusebius, the bishop of Caesarea (from the fourth century).[8] The fragment of Papias' work, "*Exposition of the Oracles of the Lord,*" (of the which we only have a few passages that were also conserved by Eusebius of Caesarea), says the following:

> *And the presbyter said this. Mark having become the interpreter of Peter, wrote down accurately whatsoever he remembered. It was not, however, in exact order that he related the sayings or deeds of Christ. For he neither heard the Lord nor accompanied Him. But afterwards, as I said, he accompanied Peter, who accommodated his instructions to the necessities [of his hearers], but with no intention of giving a regular narrative of the Lord's sayings. Wherefore Mark made no mistake in thus writing some things as he remembered them.*

---

[8] Eusebius of Caesarea, *The History of the Church* or *Historia Eclesiástica* (in Greek, Ἐκκλησιαστικὴ ἱστορία)

*For one thing, he took special care, not to omit anything he had heard, and not to put anything fictitious into the statements.*[9],

All the testimonies after Papias identify Mark as the author of this Gospel. We can find the recognition of his authorship in the writings of: Justin Martyr, the Muratorian Canon, Irenaeus, (*who was a disciple of Polycarp, who, in his day, was a disciple of the Apostle John*), Clement of Alexandria, Origen of Alexandria, and the church fathers of the following centuries such as Eusebius and others. These patriarchs confessed and corroborated the same testimonies of Mark's authorship of the Gospel that holds his name.[10]

Therefore, with this consistency of testimony from trustworthy sources, we can rest in the orthodoxy of the authenticity of Mark's authorship as a fact. It is also indispensable to mention that all the patriarchs that we have mentioned affirm that the Apostol Peter was the principal source of information that Mark utilized in his Gospel.

## Details of the Gospel of Mark

Revelations 4:7 describes the cherubim around the Throne of God as beings with four faces: The face of a lion, the face of a calf, the face of a man, and a face like a flying eagle. Traditionally,

---

[9] Church Fathers: Fragments of Papias - New Advent, http://www.newadvent.org/fathers/0125.htm (accessed April 16, 2019).

[10] Rafael Sanz. Escritura Sagrada, https://rsanzcarrera2.wordpress.com/2007/08/12/Mark-autor-fuentes-externas/. (Accessed el 05/02/2019).

scholars say that these four faces represent the four Gospels and describe the character and message of each one. You can see this analogy in the representation of one of the Gospels with these creatures in cathedrals all around Europe.

The creature representing the Gospel of Mark is the calf; this is a beast of labor and service. The Gospel of Mark teaches us about Jesus as the Servant of God. We know that the Gospel of Mark was written to the Roman Believers, and it is believed that Mark wrote this Gospel in Rome. For this reason, we see the Gospel of Mark is a book full of things that Jesus did, transitioning rapidly from one event to another. We also find the Lord so busy that in Mark 3:20, it says that Jesus and his disciples had no time to eat.

One of the key words that we find, about forty times in this Gospel, is the Greek word, *euthéos*, (εὐθέως) which means, "*after that*" or "*immediately*". We find a Christ busy as the Servant of God and fulfilling His purpose on the Earth as the Messiah of the Father. In this Gospel, the emphasis is in the Works of Christ more than in His words.

## Simon Peter's Influence

When Jesus first called him, he addressed him as Simon, son of Jonah. "*And he brought him to Jesus. And when Jesus beheld him, he said, thou art Simon the son of Jonah: thou shalt be called Cephas, which is by interpretation, A stone...*" (John 1:42 JUB).

As mentioned, it is believed by many scholars that the Apostol Peter was the principal source of information for this Gospel. Many also consider that the idea of the Gospel of Mark is an early testimony of the Apostol Peter. Furthermore, some prefer to think of the title of this book as, "The Gospel According to Simon Peter."[11]

Although all the Gospels have details that the others overlook, the undertones of this Gospel give evidence that can easily be identified as an eyewitness account of the author. As I develop my argument, I will present, in an orderly fashion, reasons that Peter would have had so much influence over the life and writings of John Mark.

Another indication of Peter's influence in this book is the fact that Peter's native language was Aramaic, and Mark contains more phrases in Aramaic than any other Gospel. We have such phrases as:

- *"Boanerges"* (Mark 3:17);
- *Talitha cumi* or *Talitha, koum* (5:41),
- *Corban* (7:11),
- *Ephphatha, Efata, Efatá, or, Effatá* [ἐφφαθά] (7:34), and
- *Abba* (14:36).

As I have mentioned, Mark wrote his Gospel to the Romans, a hardworking people, diligent and oriented towards accomplishments. However, the nature of the church in Rome has long been debated. Was it a Jewish congregation, or, was it a church of a mixture of Jews, with a majority of Roman Gentiles that,

---

[11] Bob Utley, *The Gospel According to Peter: Mark and 1 & 2 Peter*, Marshall, TX: Bible Lessons International. 2012.

beforehand, were considered God-Fearers?[12],[13] Dr. Bob Utley says that, during the period in which the Roman Emperor Claudius expelled all of the Jews from Rome, the church became naturally dominated by God Fearing Gentiles that had believed in Christ. When the Jews returned, there was a time of adjustment that the Apostles had to monitor.[14]

Mark's Gospel does not contain a genealogy, because the Romans held no interest in the genealogy of some Jew from Palestine. The Romans were interested in works and actions. They wanted to know precisely what was it that Jesus did that made him so appealing. Therefore, we have this strong emphasis on Christ being presented as the Servant of God.

---

[12] Acts 13:16 *"So Paul stood up and motioning with his hand said: "Men of Israel and you who fear God, listen."*

[13] Jesús Mosterín. *Los cristianos: Historia del pensamiento*. Madrid: Alianza Editorial 2010:

*During the eras of Julius Cesar and of Octavius Caesar Augustus, the Jewish population increased not only demographically, but also because of the act of active and successful proselytism among the Gentiles from the broad Hellenistic cultures and societies.*

*There were two stages in this approach to Judaism among the Gentiles. The proselyte (newcomer) was a Gentile that had completely embraced Judaism, having submitted to circumcision, had accepted all the ritual regulations of the Judaic law. Upon completing this rite of passage, they became a wholly accepted member of the synagogue.*

*Many Gentiles felt drawn by the Jewish doctrines of monotheism, and came faithfully to the synagogue, but did not submit to the ritual of circumcision or necessarily accept the rules of conduct with all their details (referring to, for example, the strict observation of the Sabbath, certain dietary laws, or purification rituals). They called them God-Fearers, in Greek phoboumenoi (from phobéō, to fear) and in Latin, metuentes (from metuere, to fear). The God-Fearers were not legally considered Jews, but they helped in the synagogues and formed a reservoir of potential proselytes.*

[14] Bob Utley, *The Letter to the Romans: The Gospel According to Paul: Romans.* Marshall, TX: Bible Lessons International. 2015.

Once again, I must direct your attention to the linguistics of Mark's Gospel when we see how Latin terms and phrases are used. However, this time we must defer to the Greek to find these Latinisms because of the way that many English Bibles translate these Latin words and phrases. Sometimes they will use the terms directly; other times they might use an understandable English term. We find that this Gospel has more Latin words and phrases than any other. Therefore, by observing this usage of Latin words and terminologies that we readily find in the Greek manuscripts, I want to point out another indication that Mark wrote his Gospel to minister to the Roman mentality. We have words such as:

- *Census* (κῆνσος, "poll tax" 12:14),
- *Centurio* (κεντυρίων, "Centurion" 15:39, 44, 45),
- *Denarius* (δηνάριον, a Roman coin, 12:15),
- *Legio* (λεγιών, "legion" 5:9, 15),
- *Modius* (μόδιος, "peck measure" 4:21),
- *Praetorium* (πραιτώριον, "governor's official residence" 15:16),
- *Quadrans* (κοδράντης, a Roman coin, 12:42),
- *Sextarius* (ξέστης, quart measure, "pitcher" 7:4),
- *Speculator* (σπεκουλάτωρ, "executioner" 6:27), and
- *Flagellum* (φραγελλόω, "to flog" 15:15).[15]

---

[15] Dr. Rod Decker, Dr. Wayne Slusser, *Gospel of Mark/Latinisms in Mark's Gospel*, NT Resources, http://ntresources.com/blog/?p=1205 (accessed 04/17/2019)

Clement of Alexandria [*Titus Flavius Clemens*] (150-215 A.D.) in his work titled *Hypotyposis*, refers to a tradition passed on from "the elders since the beginning":

> *... however, the light of Peters preaching shined in the minds of those that heard him to such an extent that they were not satisfied with hearing it only once, or with unwritten oral teaching of the Divine message. So that with diverse pleadings they implored Mark, (of whom it was believed had written the Gospel and was Peter's companion) insisting that he set down in writing leaving them a keepsake of that which they had received orally. They did not leave let relax until he finished, and this became the text called the Gospel of Mark.*[16]

We received an additional aspect from Eusebius when he wrote in concerning Mark's work with Peter:

> *... the Gospel according to St. Mark has the following origin: When Peter preached the Word publicly in Rome... those present, which were many, exhorted Mark, who had accompanied him for much time... to put into writing these words. When Peter learned of this... he did not disagree.*[17]

---

[16] Ecclesiastical History, Book II Chapter XV
[17] Ecclesiastical History, Book IV Chapter XIV

This work is essential because Clement appears to have a source that provides us with a slightly different perspective.

Eusebius quoted an evangelical commentary written by Origen that, also attributes the Gospel of Mark to Peter:

> *... The second is from Mark, who wrote it following the instructions of Peter, who, in his universal epistle, recognizes as his son saying: "She who is at Babylon, who is likewise chosen, sends you greetings, and so does Mark, my son"* 1º Peter 5:13.[18]

Finally, I will mention the "Anti-Marcionite Prologue" of the Latin Bibles that are dated from around the fourth century or before. There are three of these "prologues" of the Gospels.[19] However, in the context of our argument, the prologue of the Gospel of Mark is particularly interesting. It says: *"After the death of Peter, he [Mark] wrote this same Gospel in the regions of Italy."*[20]

## Historical Clues and Indications

We catch many historical glimpses of Mark and his testimony. We have evidence that he made missionary trips into

---

[18] Historia Eclesiástica Libro VI Chapter XXV

[19] Bob Utley, *The Gospel According to Peter: Mark and 1 & 2 Peter*, pgs. 4-5, Marshall, TX: Bible Lessons International, 2012.

[20] J. Warner Wallace, *Is Mark's Gospel an Early Memoir of the Apostle Peter?* Cold-Case Christianity.com. https://coldcasechristianity.com/writings/is-marks-gospel-an-early-memoir-of-the-apostle-peter/. July 25, 2018. (accessed el 04/17/2019)

Alexandria, a renowned city of commerce and study, to preach the Gospel of Christ. He planted a strong church there that today is known as the Coptic Orthodox Church. According to their tradition, the Coptic Church finds its origin in the preaching of Mark, the author of the second Gospel in the first century, when he took the Gospel to Egypt during the time of Emperor Nero.

Today, the Coptic Orthodox Church has more than seventy million followers worldwide. This religious organization maintains that the Apostle John Mark established this work in Alexandria, Egypt, in the year 42 of the first century. Therefore, historically, the Coptic Church, founded in Africa in the first century, is older than the Catholic Church.

Mark, the valiant servant of God, died as a martyr in Alexandria. He was killed during a pagan feast by an angry mob that had gathered in the Temple of Serapis.[21] Mark was celebrating the Resurrection of Christ when the angry throng fell upon him and the Believers that were with him. Consequently, he was captured and dragged with ropes down the principal streets of the city. Afterward, most probably during the triumphal procession of Serapis, he was, once again, dragged through the streets until he died.

### Who was John Mark?

The best way to begin a systematic study of any book or passage of Scripture is to do a Biblical and historical study of

---

[21] The Serapeum of Alexandria was the product of the syncretism of Egyptian and Greek mythologies. The Temple of Serapis was in Alexandria, Egypt.

the author. This study can only be done if the author is known, because it is clear, that the authorship of some of the books of the Bible is nearly impossible to determine. Nevertheless, this is not our case with the Gospel of Mark.

To do this with the Biblical investigation in this study, we have eight explicit references of Mark in the book of Acts, as well as in the epistles. Also, there is a strong possibility of a reference to the author in the same Gospel that bears his name. So, we want to look at verses that identify this evangelist and other passages that give us much more information as to his identity, background, history, character, and personality.

The first place we find him mentioned by name is in Acts 12:12. *"And when he had considered this thing, he went to the house of Mary, the mother of John, whose surname was Mark, where many were gathered together praying..."* (KJ21). Fortunately, when we find him mentioned for the first time, we also find the name of his mother, Mary.

After this, we find Mark mentioned by name in Acts 12:25, Acts 15:37, Acts 15:39, 2nd Timothy 4:11, Philemon 1:24, and 1st Peter 5:13. From everything that we know and can confirm, there is only one person in the Scriptures that bears the name or surname of Mark, or, as we know him in Acts, John Mark.

John Mark is a compound name taken from two languages. This practice was common in the polyglot world in which he lived. John was his Hebrew name, (וְיהוֹנָתָן) (pronounced: *yehônâthân*), which means, *"Jehovah has given, graced or favored"*.[22] This was the name of at least fourteen Hebrews in

---

[22] Brown, Driver, Briggs. H3110 A Related Word by BDB/Strong's Number: a form of H3076

the Old Testament.[23] Even though John was his Hebrew name, Mark was his Roman name. As we will see, this was normal in the Galilean and Judean regions during the first century because of the pluricultural ambience that prevailed in that part of the Roman Empire. This also facilitated life for people that moved through cosmopolitan ambiences. We will see this in more detail in another chapter.

In John Mark's case, his Jewish name was eventually all but forgotten as per the references to him in Scripture, as he is later known only as Mark. We can see that this was not atypical for renowned personalities in the New Testament. For example, many times, if we mention Joseph of Cyprus, many of today's faithful Believers would not know who he is (see Acts 4:36).

John Mark eventually left his Hebrew name behind, because he had dedicated his life to working to reach people for Christ that were outside of the Judean-Hebrew ambiance and culture in which he was raised. Just as Saul (*Shaul - Hebrew*) and Silouanos[24] did, they found that it was much easier to utilize a Greek or Latin name to facilitate communication and the

---

[23] Jonathan, the son of Gershom, the son of Manasseh (Judges 18:30); Jonathan the son of Saul (I Samuel 14:1); Jonathan the son of Abiathar (II Samuel 15:27); Jonathan the son of Shimea the brother of David (II Samuel 21:21); of the sons of Jashen, Jonathan (II Samuel 23:32); Jonathan the son of Abiathar the priest (Iº Kings 1:42); Johanan the son of Careah (II Reyes 25:23); And the sons of Jada the brother of Shammai; Jether, and Jonathan (I Chronicles 2:32); Jonathan the son of Shage the Hararite, (I Chronicles 11:34); Jehonathan the son of Uzziah (I Chronicles 27:25); Jonathan David's uncle (I Chronicles 27:32); Jehonathan the Levite (II Chronicles 17:8); Jonathan the son of Asahel (Ezra 10:15); Jonathan, the son of Shemaiah (Nehemiah 12:35); Jonathan the scribe: (Jeremiah 37:15); Johanan (*Jehovah has favored*) and Jonathan (*Jehovah has given*) the sons of Kareah (Jeremiah 40:8); *There are, at least, five more of undetermined origin.*

[24] Strong's G4610: Σιλουανός of Latin origin; "silvan"; Silvanus,

pronunciation of their names for the people to whom they ministered.

My wife's name is Guillermina, but when we minister to people that only speak English, we always introduce her simply as Gina. It's just that it's not only painful to see people mangle her name or suffer trying to pronounce it correctly; it's just plain easier for everyone to give her an English name and be done with it.

In this study, I want to help us understand these notably influential New Testament personalities with sharper clarity, and to be able to see and understand them from the perspective of their Biblical and situational context as we read about them in the Scriptures. We must understand the things that separate us from the world in which Mark and his contemporaries lived.

# Chapter 2

# INFLUENCES THAT PROVOKE AN EISEGESIS AND NOT AN EXEGESIS

**An Exegetical Bridge**

We must be conscious of the fact that our culture conditions our perceptions and our way of thinking. In this case, we have today, a historical and cultural influence that the people in the first century did not have. I want to provide a bridge that would span the time between the culture and cosmovision of Mark's day and those of ours. Added to John Mark's time and cultural distinctions is another very evident feature that separates us. I am talking about the philological aspects[25] of the places in which he and his contemporaries lived and worked.

Therefore, in the development of the foundation of my argument, we will observe the various facets of these issues. Some of these matters we will view briefly, while others we will study in greater detail.

In the first part of this study, we will concentrate, primarily, on marriage and celibacy. Counted among the barriers that

---

[25] Merriam-Webster's Collegiate Dictionary, 11th edition. April 23, 2008. Springfield, MA: Merriam-Webster, Inc., **Philology** (noun): *Linguistics - especially historical and comparative linguistics; the study of human speech especially as the vehicle of literature and as a field of study that sheds light on cultural history.*

impede a clear comprehension of several of the features of our theme, is the concept of the sanctity of our marital relationships, and the procreation of children. A correct understanding of this simple truth can change the focus of the orientation that one might hold of our study.

In the same way, we must understand the struggles of life, emotional situations, relationship dynamics, and other vicissitudes that we all have in common, and that unites us. The incidences of which I speak are things as simple as our humanity, frailty, and our everyday family and work relationships. We will study the environment of the Christ, Mark, and albeit briefly, other protagonists of the Bible so that we might gain an understanding and relate to the reality of their world, the people that surrounded them, and their families.

For this reason, I will dedicate several pages of this work to the ideas associated with the command of God and what the Bible says about marriage, the sexual relationship in marriage and the servants of God. I will also give a brief history of the fluctuating criterion held on this subject throughout the history of the church. I will do this to build the foundation of our argument about our person of interest; John Mark, his life, and his family.

## It Was Very Good

It is indispensable that we examine the elements that, in general, have influenced our cultural mentality, and at times even our theological perspective. Being that many, without knowing it, or that are unwilling to admit it have been influenced by the Catholic concept of holiness and of holy people in the Scriptures. We are not able to see them as normal human beings just as we are, with the same emotional and relational conditions and situations as ours. Nevertheless, this is just how the Bible exhorts us to see them.

The Apostle James in chapter five of his epistle directs our attention to the open humanity of two worthy figures: Elijah and Job.[26] About Elijah it says:

> *Elijah was a man of like passions with us, and he prayed fervently that it might not rain; and it rained not on the earth for three years and six months. And he prayed again; and the heaven gave rain, and the earth brought forth her fruit.* (James 5:17-18 ASV)

This passage implies that all the Biblical personalities, our heroes, were merely men and women that loved God; and, just like us, at times they did so imperfectly. They were just like us

---

[26] *10 Take, brethren, for an example of suffering and of patience, the prophets who spake in the name of the Lord. 11 Behold, we call them blessed that endured: ye have heard of the patience of Job, and have seen the end of the Lord, how that the Lord is full of pity, and merciful. 12 But above all things, my brethren, swear not, neither by the heaven, nor by the earth, nor by any other oath: but let your yea be yea, and your nay, nay; that ye fall not under judgment. 13 Is any among you suffering? let him pray. Is any cheerful? let him sing praise. 14 Is any among you sick? let him call for the elders of the church; and let them pray over him, anointing him with oil in the name of the Lord: 15 and the prayer of faith shall save him that is sick, and the Lord shall raise him up; and if he have committed sins, it shall be forgiven him. 16 Confess therefore your sins one to another, and pray one for another, that ye may be healed. The supplication of a righteous man availeth much in its working. 17 Elijah was a man of like passions with us, and he prayed [e]fervently that it might not rain; and it rained not on the earth for three years and six months. 18 And he prayed again; and the heaven gave rain, and the earth brought forth her fruit.* (James 5:10-18 ASV)

in their humanity, yet at the same time, they gave everything to Him. As it has been said, the question is not, "*Where is the God of Elijah?*" Instead, we should ask, "*Where are God's Elijahs?*"

The Apostle Paul reaffirmed James' conviction by saying, "*No temptation [regardless of its source] has overtaken or enticed you that is not common to human experience [nor is any temptation unusual or beyond human resistance] ...*" (1 Corinthians 10:13 AMP). In the same manner, the author of the epistle of Hebrews confirmed the same mentality saying:

> *For we do not have a High Priest Who is unable to understand and sympathize and have a shared feeling with our weaknesses and infirmities and liability to the assaults of temptation, but One Who has been tempted in every respect as we are, yet without sinning...* (Amplified Bible AMPC)

## The Beginning of the Departure

We should have this clear, that the Apostle Paul warned us prophetically of a significant deviation that would prove to be a stumbling block for the church, and promote the departure of some from the faith in I Timothy 4:1-3 saying:

> *Now the Spirit speaks expressly, that in the latter times some shall depart from the faith, giving heed to seducing spirits, and doctrines of devils; Speaking lies in hypocrisy; having their conscience seared with a hot iron; Forbidding to marry, and*

> *commanding to abstain from meats, which God hath created to be received with thanksgiving of them which believe and know the truth.* (BRG)

The sobering part of this warning that I want to point out is the portion where it says: *"Forbidding to marry…"* The Catholic church presents, as dogma, that holy people are so close to God that they no need or desires for natural or mundane things such as marriage, or the sexual relationship found in marriage. It is taught that these saints are so disconnected from this life that they do not feel the longing, nor do they have any need for any of these natural desires.

Nevertheless, in their correct place, these elements are a part of the spiritual and organic design of God and have been created to be the work and the will of God for our lives. This organic design is also one way He would manifest Himself in the lives of these Biblical protagonists. Being in Christ and walking in His will, these very elements with their desires and functions do not impede His work of holiness in us, because God Himself has created it to be this way.

I must state here that what I am indicating concerning someone remaining unmarried, or if they decide to marry is completely a matter of that individual's intimate and personal decision. I reiterate that this decision is extremely personal and pertains solely between the Believer and their Creator. The Apostle Paul, a single man, said, *"Don't we have the right to be accompanied by a believing wife like the other apostles, the Lord's brothers, and Cephas?"* (1 Corinthians 9:5 CSB).

Biblical teaching is completely open concerning this personal decision for any Believer if they choose not to marry (1 Corinthians 7:1, 6-9, 25-40). However, it was also the Apostle Paul that taught us that, those that taught forced celibacy, were teaching a Satanic doctrine (1 Timothy 4:1-3).

In 1 Timothy 3:1-2, Paul wrote of the qualifications that a candidate for a bishopric need to fulfill if they were married. In these requirements, there is no demand that a person be married to be a bishop, but that, if the candidate was a married person, then these are the requirements that they must fulfill in their marriage.

> *This saying is reliable: if anyone has a goal to be a supervisor*[27] *in the church, they want a good thing. 2 So the church's supervisor must be without fault. They should be faithful to their spouse, sober, modest, and honest. They should show hospitality and be skilled at teaching;* (1 Timothy 3:1-2 CEB).

## Holiness and the Eucharist

Nonetheless, because of the ideology that all these desires are carnal, thus contrary to the will of God brings us to the reason that the Catholic clergy must take the vow of celibacy. They must prove that they are holier than the laity; or, that is to say, holier than the rest of the congregation that is not

---

[27] Strong's: G1984 (ἐπισκοπή) From G1980; inspection (for relief); by implication superintendence; specifically, the Christian "episcopate": - the office of a "bishop", bishoprick, visitation, bishop, overseer.

ministry. This concept is promoted to prove that they have been counted worthy of being used by God for the Eucharist.

To underscore this point, the Catholic theologian, Antonio Orozco-Delclós, in his brief, but well written an interesting monograph titled, *"Celibacy, Priesthood, and the* Eucharist" said:

> *Everything is focused and concentrated on the Eucharist. It is superior to all passion, and every great passion finds its maximum and definite meaning in it. In one way, the first that is attracted and immersed in the Mystery is the priest that celebrates the Eucharistic Sacrifice, the Holy Mass.*
>
> *For this reason, as I see it, Pope Benedict pronounced the final word, after a multitude of attempts throughout the history of theology, in the Closure of the recent Synod. The words are these, brief, concise, yet formidable: «Over the Eucharistic mystery, celebrated and worshipped, is founded the vow of celibacy that the presbyters have received as a precious gift and sign of indivisible love to God and our neighbor»* [Homily of the Closure of the Synod of the bishops and of the Year of the Eucharist (23.X.2005)].[28]

Reverend Orozco-Delclós continues by saying:

---

[28] Antonio Orozco-Delclós, *Celibato Sacerdotal y Eucaristía*, Arvo Net (06 noviembre, 2005). http://arvo.net/sacramento-del-orden/celibato-sacerdotal-y-eucaristia/gmx-niv503-con16748.htm. (accessed 12/31/2018).

*Now then, to overcome all the possible difficulties that might arise to live faithfully to this commitment, we just need to remember: How is any great passion overcome? Answer: it is done with an even greater passion. The priest is the witness of the existence of the strongest of all human passions, though these are seemingly invincible, and even though they might result in violence at one point in our human existence.*

*As John Paul II noted, «the maximum reason for the discipline of celibacy cannot be founded on the field of psychology, sociology, history, or the judiciary, but, essentially, in the pastoral and theological fields, in the ministerial charisma.» Neither can it be founded in the fact that «there is yet much to be done,» the which is true – and it will be accomplished, if the priest is faithful to his priestly «inner self.»*[29]

## The Roman Empire and the Roman Catholic Church

Now then, it is necessary to pause here before we proceed with my clarification concerning Peter. I want to present you with a straightforward question: If the Catholics present Peter as the first pope, then how is it that Peter was a married man when the Roman Catholic institution demands celibacy of its

---

[29] Ibid.

clergy? From where did this concept of celibacy come to hold such an influence in the Christian mentality?

Also, and, I admit that this is a point of minor importance, it is interesting to see how antithetical it is that this institution is called the "Roman Catholic Church," when the Roman Empire looked upon celibacy as an aberration. The repugnance against celibacy was to such an extent that they had a law called, la *Lex Papia Poppaea*.[30]

The Lex Papia et Poppaea was a Roman law introduced in 9 A.D., to encourage and strengthen marriage.[31] It included provisions against adultery and celibacy and complemented and supplemented Augustus' *Lex Julia de Maritandis Ordinibus* of 18 B.C., and the *Lex Iulia de Adulteriis Coercendis* of 17 B.C. The law was introduced by the suffect consuls of that year, Marcus Papius Mutilus and Quintus Poppaeus Secundus, although they were unmarried.[32],[33]

They charged fines and imposed other penalties upon celibates or single adults that refused to marry after a certain age. They believed, (*ironically, considering just how libertine the Romans were*), that such acts of celibacy promoted, or gave place to unbridled adultery and fornication which, in turn,

---

[30] George Long, "Lex Papia Poppaea"; A Dictionary of Greek and Roman Antiquities. Public Domain. John Murray, London, 1875 p. 691–692. Personal Commentary: *I do not have an opinion for or against this law. That is not my purpose. I am simply registering historical data in the building of my argument.*

[31] Susan Treggiari, "*Roman Marriage: Iusti Coniuges from the Time of Cicero to the Time of Ulpian*". (1993) Oxford and New York, Clarendon Press.

[32] George Long, "Lex Papia Poppaea"; A Dictionary of Greek and Roman Antiquities. Public Domain. John Murray, London, 1875 p. 691–692.

[33] Revolvy. Lex Papia Poppaea. https://www.revolvy.com/page/Lex-Papia-Poppaea (accessed 04/18/2019).

weakened the institution of the family, and as a result, would weaken the entire empire. Added to this, as the families of the plebe procreated children, the empire was guaranteed the growth of faithful families dedicated to Rome, because these children would be natural citizens of the empire. The only exception to this law were the Vestal Virgins.

To understand the context of Rome and the Vestal Virgins, it is necessary to know something of the virgin goddess Vesta, and her vestal followers:

> *The pure and immaculate Vesta, also known as Hestia in Greece, was the goddess of fire and the family chimney. Gradually, she became the protecting goddess of Rome whose flame represented the well-being of the state, that is to say "la res publica" ... she was considered the protector of humanity... She was courted by Apollos and Neptune, but she preferred to remain pure and virgin... This purity was represented by the holy fire – that the Romans considered an emblem of the flame of life that burns in the breast of humankind, thanks to Vesta ... Her feast day was the Vestalia, and ... was one of the most extravagant and popular among the Roman populous. It was the unequivocal sign of love and worship for this goddess.*[34]

---

[34] Las Vírgenes Vestales (The Vestal Virgins). https://www.imperivm.org/articulos/vestales.html Translated (accessed 03/02/2019 - permission was solicited).

I think that this is the very same concept in the Catholic church even to this day with their worship of the Virgin Mary. The goddess Vesta was worshipped for her virginity, and this is what, in part, gave her such power. The Catholics venerate Mary, the mother of Jesus for her perpetual virginity. Thus, according to their dogma, this perpetual virginity is what is purported to make her pure and holy in God's sight.

What is also interesting, and almost antithetical, is the connection between this Roman law prohibiting celibacy associated with the idea of the increase of the citizens of Rome by way of the natural numerical growth of the families. Consider this, as the Catholic institution prohibits contraceptives, Catholic families naturally grow. As is logical, if the families grow, so too does the church. This prohibition, though in some ways devious, is a brilliant concept, for ideally, these children are raised in the church and grow to have a natural affinity and dedication to their religious upbringing.

### The Catholic Influence

Though it seems to be a simple snare to avoid, it is surprising to learn just how subtle this divergence has been, and at how high a cost. For this Catholic influence has clouded our perspective of the realities, or the natural possibilities of the Biblical characters that we, so often, rightly esteem as heroes.

This influence taints our perception to the point that we often find these beloved Biblical personalities distantly removed from our everyday reality. Unless it is explicitly mentioned, to think that they would have had wives with whom they had sexual relations and had children seems inconceivable. At times, in our minds, such a concept borders on the absurd and unthinkable. In some cases, even among very religious Protestants, this is even close to blasphemy.

For these, to teach that these valiant Biblical leaders were people with desires, anxieties, needs, passions, worries and everyday struggles just as we have, would lower them to our carnal level. Nevertheless, that is how it was. As I have said, they were merely human beings just like us, that loved God and walked faithfully with Him, paying attention to His voice, and obeying Him.

They did not see miracles, nor did they experience the marvels of which we read in the Scriptures every day. However, when God moved with His wondrous power, they were meticulous to register these works in their writings, detailing many of the miraculous and supernatural events that they saw and experienced. The Apostle John told us hyperbolically in his Gospel that: *"... there are also many other things Yeshua did; and if they were all to be recorded, I don't think the whole world could contain the books that would have to be written!"* (John 21:25 CJB).

Having said this, if we are going to learn from this conversation, we must first see how the concept that to live as a married couple, and procreating children is equivalent to being carnally minded entered our ideology. From where did it come? How is it that we have been so influenced as to force an eisegesis on specific passages and Biblical characters?

I will reiterate and say, that it began with specific concepts from the Catholic church that have forced evolution of thought by way of hundreds of years of slight alterations of untouchable Biblical truths. Now then, I do not pretend to be exhaustive, in any way, with this topic. I deem it necessary to touch it momentarily to give clarity to the subject matter at hand. Therefore, I will give a brief historical review of precisely how this mentality infiltrated the perspective of today's church:

## Celibacy

The concept of celibacy is not original with Christianity or Catholicism. Long before this notion entered Catholicism, it was practiced in Buddhism.

> The historical Buddha insisted on celibacy for monks and nuns because suffering was caused by ignorant craving and because sexual relations encouraged attachment to the world. Both functioned as obstacles to mental concentration. Monastic rules helped one to comprehend the reason for the essential role of celibacy in the quest for liberation. Buddhist practice became more complex with later developments, such as Tibetan Buddhism, which witnessed some schools insisting on celibacy, while others allowed sexual intercourse within a ritualistic context for advanced practitioners, and other schools approved a married clergy.[35]

---

[35] Carl Olson, *Celibacy and Religious Traditions*, Published to Oxford Scholarship Online: January 2008. http://www.oxfordscholarship.com/view/10.1093/acprof:oso/9780195306316.001.0001/acprof-9780195306316-chapter-11

In the second and third centuries, the age of Gnosticism entered the church teaching that light and spirit were good, and that darkness and material things were evil. Furthermore, it assimilated marriage under the same perspective saying that a person could not be married and be perfect. Nevertheless, most of the leaders of the church were married men.

The beginning of the Catholic decree was in the fourth century, in the Synod of Elvira (*Concilium Eliberritanum*) in the year 306 A.D. It was the first synod that proclaimed what is called the 33rd Canon and was the first synod held in Spain. This canon introduced the first law of celibacy. It says: "Any priest that sleeps with his wife the night before he has to give mass, will be expelled from his position."[36]

After this, in 325 A.D., the Council of Nicaea was held. In this synod, the 3rd Canon was decreed. This canon says that once a priest has been ordained, they are prohibited from marrying.[37]

In the year 401 A.D., Augustine of Hippo wrote: "*There is nothing more powerful that can vilify the spirit of a man than the caresses of a woman.*"[38]

From there forward, everything like water followed its course downhill and against all that which was ordained and approved by God in holy matrimony for the servants of God as it is written in the Word of God. It has gone to the point that, as

---

[36] Philip Schaff (1819-1893), *History of the Christian Church, vol. II: Ante-Nicene Christianity A.D. 100–325*, §33, pg. 256. Grand Rapids, MI: Christian Classics Ethereal Library, 1882.

[37] Enciclopedia Católica Online. *Primer Concilio de Nicea*, Translated by Juan Ramón Martínez Maurica. L H M. http://ec.aciprensa.com/wiki/Primer_Concilio_de_Nicea. (Accessed el 18/12/2018).

[38] Agustin (Bishop of Hippo), *Celibacy and Nicolaism or Concubinato*, The History of the Catholic Church. De Constantino al Concilio de Trento (313 - 1545).

recently as May 28, 2010, when an official article was published[39] written by Sandro Magister, the official secretary of the press for the Vatican, titled, *Eunuchs for the Kingdom of Heaven. The Argument over Celibacy*. Magister says:

> *Throughout the first millennium and afterward, in the Church, the celibacy of the clergy was properly understood as "continence." Meaning as complete renunciation, after ordination, of conjugal life, even for those who had previously been married.*
>
> *The ordination of married men, in fact, was a common practice, also documented by the New Testament. But in the Gospel, one reads that Peter, after his call to be an apostle, "left everything." And Jesus said that there are some who even leave "wives or children" for the Kingdom of God."*[40]

This is precisely the kind of eisegesis that infuses the mindset that has managed to permeate Evangelical theology. Subtly, it has slithered in and inspired the struggle or the open rejection of the concept of family relations among the Biblical personalities of our general subject matter; That of John Mark, Peter, and others.

---

[39] At the foot of the page of the article is the Vatican's approval of this essay.

[40] Sandro Magister, *Eunuchs for the Kingdom of Heaven. The Argument over Celibacy*. News, analysis, and documents on the Catholic Church, by Sandro Magister, Rome. May 28, 2010. http://chiesa.espresso.repubblica.it/articolo/1343466bdc4.html?eng=y. (accessed 01/20/2019).

## A Logical and Natural Part of the Perfect Plan of God

Though it might seem rudimentary, I find it necessary to underscore the point that marriage is a Divine act, blessed and approved of God. Hebrews 13:4 says: *"Marriage is honorable in every respect; and, in particular, sex within marriage is pure. But God will indeed punish fornicators and adulterers."* (CJB)

Biblically, there is no doubt that God approves of marriage for all of humanity. It is also clear that this includes God's people in general and, in the Old Testament, for the priests and Levites in particular. From the beginning, it is irrefutable that God created marriage and He sanctified it. In fact, the first commandment that we find registered in the Scriptures is that of procreation.

> *So, God created humans to be like himself; he made men and women. 28 God gave them his blessing and said: Have a lot of children! Fill the earth with people and bring it under your control. Rule over the fish in the ocean, the birds in the sky, and every animal on the earth...* (Genesis 1:27-28 CEV)

Someone might claim that God blessed Adam's marital relationship because it occurred before The Fall. Nevertheless, even in The Fall and amid the declaration of the resulting curses and the expulsion from Eden, God manifested His steadfast love by giving the first prophetic promise of the coming of the Messiah, and His victory over Satan by way of the act of procreation when He said. *"And I will put enmity between thee and the woman, and between thy seed and her seed; he shall crush thy head, and thou shalt crush his heel."* (Genesis 3:15 DARBY).

As stated, this is the first Messianic prophecy, and it gives the promise of the coming of the Messiah. However, it does not say when He will come, but that He will arrive in an undetermined point sometime in the future.

After Genesis 3:15, we have the Word of God to Abraham in multiple occasions[41] telling him that, by way of a sexual relationship with his wife in his ripe old age, would be how his blessing would come. It is also manifest that by his seed, come not only the nation of Israel but also the promised Messiah.

> *Now the promises were spoken to Abraham and to his seed. He does not say [in Gen 13:15] "and to seeds", as-though speaking in reference to many; but as-though speaking in reference to one, "and to your seed"— who is Christ.* (Galatians 3:16 DLNT).

Now, merely by a logical conclusion, we can see in Matthew 1:17, that the Messiah came forty-two generations after this promise. *"So, all the generations, from Abraham to David, are fourteen generations. And from David to the transmigration of Babylon, are fourteen generations: and from the transmigration of Babylon to Christ are fourteen generations."* (DRA)

---

[41] Genesis 12:2; 13:16; 15:13-18; 17:5-10; 17:15-21; 18:9-16; 21:1-3.

## Moses and the Levites

We know that Moses was married and had children when God called him, and when He was using him (Exodus 2:21-22; Number 12:1). We also know that Leviticus chapter 21 gives specific instructions to the Levites that were priests on how, and with whom they should marry. This chapter specifies the characteristics of the woman with whom a priest should marry (Leviticus 21:7).

Even still, in an apparent antithetical command to this instruction, God directed Hosea to marry a prostitute. He ordered him to do so as an illustration of how the nations of Israel and Judah were married to the Lord, yet were unfaithful to Him, even though His love for them was unwavering.

## Jeremiah and Ezekiel

In the same illustrative manner, but inversely, God commanded Jeremiah not to marry so that he could illustrate his message in a different way:

> *The Lord's message came to me: 2 "Jeremiah, you must not get married. You must not have sons or daughters in this place." This is what the Lord says about the sons and daughters who are born in the land of Judah and about their mothers and fathers: "They will die from terrible disease. And no one will cry for them or bury them. Their bodies will lie on the ground like dung. Or they will die in war or*

> *starve to death. Their dead bodies will be food for the birds of the sky and the wild animals of the earth."* (Jeremiah 16:1-4 ERV)

In that verse, we see that God told Jeremiah not to marry anybody in the place where he lived. We also know that Ezekiel was married and became a widower during his ministry. *"So, I spoke to the people in the morning, and at evening my wife died. And on the next morning I did as I was commanded."* (Ezekiel 24:18 ESV).

## Abraham, "Ishmael," Isaac, and Jacob

In Exodus 3:15, God identified Himself as the God of Abraham, the God of Isaac, and the God of Jacob. One of His major works in their lives was that of procreating children for His glory and perfect will. Abraham is known as the Father of the Faith, principally, because he believed God that he would father a child with his wife Sarah, and from him, nations would be born.

> *And he brought him outside and said, "Look towards heaven, and number the stars, if you are able to number them." Then he said to him, "So shall your offspring be." And he believed the Lord, and he counted it to him as righteousness.* (Genesis 15:5-6 ESVUK)

Better still, is the fact that the promise that God gave to Abraham had a far greater reach than one single nation. God said that "nations" would come forth from him (Genesis 17:4-16). This proclamation is an indication that Ishmael was not an error that Abraham had committed in his efforts to "help" God as so many proclaim. Apart from this, Abraham's second wife, Keturah, gave birth to six sons from Abraham. Of these six, some of them also became nations. (Genesis 25:1-4)

To underscore this point, I would like to ask you something about Ishmael. How many people in the Bible did God rescue by way of direct angelic intervention? Now then, if God did not want Ishmael to exist, why did he not simply kill him as He killed two sons of Judah in Genesis 38:7-10?

> *But Er, Judah's oldest son [firstborn], did what the Lord said was evil [evil in the eyes/sight of the Lord] so the Lord killed him. 8 Then Judah said to Er's brother Onan, "Go and have sexual relations with your dead brother's wife. It is your duty to provide children for your brother in this way [raise up a seed for your brother; Deut. 25:5–10]."*

> *9 But Onan knew that the ·children [seed] would not belong to him, so when he was supposed to have sexual relations with [he went to] Tamar he did not complete the sex act [spilled his seed on the ground], making it impossible for Tamar to become pregnant and for Er to have descendants [so that he did not give a descendant/seed to his brother]. 10 The Lord was displeased by this wicked thing Onan had done [What he did was evil in the eyes/*

*sight of the Lord], so he killed Onan also.* (Genesis 38:7-10 EXB)

Nevertheless, with Ishmael, the opposite happened. God sent two angels to save Ishmael's life in Genesis 16:7-16, and Genesis 21:10-21. It is because God wanted him to live. God blessed Ishmael. That which many do not consider is that, just as God gave twelve tribes to Israel (to Jacob), He also gave twelve tribes to Ishmael in Genesis 25:12-17.

**The Messiah**

To clarify everything here concerning Ishmael, we must also take into consideration Esau's case. When we speak of Esau, we must first think of God's sovereign Messianic plan. That which is indispensable to understand when we contemplate God's purpose with Abraham's descendants is that it is centered in his Messianic vision and Master plan for humankind. The Messiah would not come through Ishmael's seed, nor any other of Abraham's children. He would only come through Isaac. The same is true when it comes to Jacob and Esau. It is not that God was saying that He did not love Esau in the verses that we read in the Scriptures when it says: *"Just as it is written: "Jacob I loved, but Esau I hated..."* (Romans 9:13 EHV).

By saying this, God was not manifesting something that would have been an open contradiction to His immutable attributes. The attribute, in this case, would be that of love, because "God is love." With this expression, it is not so much that God can love. Though we do so imperfectly, we are also capable of loving.

However, love is the essence of God's being, because God IS love. (Although, we should not confuse this concept by saying that love is God. That could prove to be a spiritually fatal error.)

I regress and reiterate because what we see in these cases is simply God's Messianic plan. God chose Isaac, the child born one hundred percent by faith, and not Ismael; He chose Jacob, and not Esau to be the progenitors of the Messiah.

Behold, the first coming of the Messiah is the primary purpose of the promise of God from the beginning until the end of this narrative. From Genesis to Malachi, the Messiah is the primary purpose of the entire Biblical discourse, and this is the principal focus of the entire Old Testament.

## Continuing with the Subject

Now then, I believe that we can agree by saying that it would be a superfluous redundancy to indicate all such similar incidents. Nevertheless, the point that I want to emphasize is that, throughout the entire Old Testament, we can see that God has worked in ways that have been redemptive and historically vital. However, I must insist that He did so primarily, by way of the conjugal act in married couples that were chosen by God to bring to pass His will on the Earth.

Therefore, all the married couples in this lineage participated in the natural procreational process, just as God established it until we come to Mary. As simple as it may seem, that which is necessary to understand is that, even though Christ was born of a virgin, Mary herself, came into this world by the natural way of the conjugal relationship of her parents.

## Chapter 3

# MARRIAGE IN THE NEW TESTAMENT

### The Family of the Lord Jesus Christ

To begin this subject, I must say once again that it is essential that we purge the influences and prejudices that can impact our way of thinking. In doing so, we will be able to read the Scriptures and come to conclusions based on an orthodox exegesis. To do this, and to take the next step to come to our principal objective, it is needful, to begin with the family of our Lord Jesus Christ, beginning with Joseph and Mary.

As per the New Testament, as I have also previously mentioned, it is evident that the birth of Jesus Christ occurred while Mary was still a virgin. Nevertheless, Mary came to us via the natural process.

### The Genealogies of Matthew and Luke

To further explain this Biblical truth, I must first present, in a summarized form, another school of thought. I am speaking of the polemical distinctions between the genealogies of the Gospels of Matthew and Luke. Though the two genealogical lines parallel each other from Abraham to David, there remain some notable differences. Nevertheless, I agree with the conservative, orthodox consensus that the Gospel of Matthew presents the genealogy of Joseph, and that of Luke presents the lineage of Mary.

Here, there is no need to re-invent the wheel. For Dr. Dave Miller, of Apologetics Press, in his brief exposition titled, "*The Genealogies of Matthew and Luke,*" does an excellent job of clarifying this school of thought in simple terms:

> *First, Matthew reported the lineage of Christ only back to Abraham; Luke traced it all the way back to Adam. Second, Matthew used the expression "begat;"[42] Luke used the expression "son of," which results in his list being a complete reversal of Matthew's. Third, the two genealogical lines parallel each other from Abraham to David. Fourth, beginning with David, Matthew traced the paternal line of descent through Solomon; Luke traced the maternal line through Solomon's brother, Nathan.*
>
> *A fifth factor that must be recognized is that the two lines (paternal and maternal) link together in the intermarriage of Shealtiel and Zerubbabel. But the linkage separates again in the two sons of Zerubbabel—Rhesa and Abiud. Sixth, the two lines come together once again for a final time in the*

---

[42] Or, "was the father of..."

marriage of Joseph and Mary. Joseph was the end of the paternal line, while Mary was the last of the maternal line as the daughter of Heli.

The reason Joseph is said to be the "son" of Heli (Mary's father) brings forth a seventh consideration: the Jewish use of "son." Hebrews used the word in at least five distinct senses:

*(1) in the sense used today of a one-generation offspring;*

*(2) in the sense of a descendant, whether a grandson or a more remote descendant many generations previous, e.g., Matthew 1:1; 21:9; 22:42 ("begat" had this same flexibility in application);*

*(3) as a son-in-law (the Jews had no word to express this concept and so just used "son"—e.g., 1 Samuel 24:16; 26:17);*

*(4) in accordance with the Levirate marriage law (Deuteronomy 25:5-10; cf. Matthew 22:24-26), a deceased man would have a son through a surrogate father who legally married the deceased man's widow (e.g., Ruth 2:20; 3:9,12; 4:3-5); and*

*(5) in the sense of a step-son who took on the legal status of his step-father—the relationship*

*sustained by Jesus to Joseph (Matthew 13:55; Mark 6:3; Luke 3:23; 4:22; John 6:42).*

*Notice carefully that Joseph was a direct-line, blood descendant of David and, therefore, of David's throne. Here is the precise purpose of Matthew's genealogy: it demonstrated Jesus' legal right to inherit the throne of David—a necessary prerequisite to authenticating His Messianic claim. However, an equally critical credential was His blood/physical descent from David—a point that could not be established through Joseph since "after His mother Mary was betrothed to Joseph, before they came together, she was found with child of the Holy Spirit" (Matthew 1:18, emp. added). This feature of Christ's Messiahship was established through His mother Mary, who was also a blood descendant of David (Luke 1:30-32). Both the blood of David and the throne of David were necessary variables to qualify and authenticate Jesus as the Messiah.*

*Once again, the Bible's intricate complexities shine forth to dispel the critic's accusations, while simultaneously demonstrating its own infallible representations. The more one delves into its intricacies and plummets its intriguing depths, the more one is driven to the inescapable conclusion that the*

> *Bible is, indeed, the Book of books—the inspired Word of God.*[43]

## Continuing with Christ's Family

Now then, after Christ's birth, Joseph and Mary were a normal married couple. (Well... as "normal" as is possible after all that just happened to you, and being that God, the Creator of the Universe just put His only begotten Son into your hands!) They were a couple that fulfilled all their natural conjugal obligations just as the Scriptures instruct us in 1st Corinthians 7:2-5.[44] The Scriptures say of Joseph and Mary:

> *When Joseph woke up, he did what the angel of the Lord had commanded him to do. He took Mary to be his wife. 25 He did not have marital relations with her before she gave birth to a son. Joseph named the child Jesus.* (Matthew 1:24-25 GW)

Christ manifested his approval of marriage when he performed his first public miracle at the wedding at Cana in Galilee in John 2:1-12. Furthermore, he showed this with his teachings

---

[43] David Miller, *The Genealogies of Matthew and Luke*. Apologetics Press, (2003) Montgomery, Alabama. https://apologeticspress.org/apcontent.aspx?category=6&article=932. (accessed 04/20/2019).

[44] (1 Corinthians 7:2-5 GNV) *Nevertheless, to avoid fornication, let every man have his wife, and let every woman have her own husband. Let the husband give unto the wife due benevolence, and likewise also the wife unto the husband. The wife hath not the power of her own body, but the husband: and likewise, also the husband hath not the power of his own body, but the wife. Defraud not one another, except it be with consent for a time, that ye may give yourselves to fasting and prayer, and again come together, that Satan tempt you not for your incontinency.*

by reiterating the blessings of Genesis 1:27. In this way, he also affirmed that marriage, in every way, is good, approved and sanctified for all the children of God when he said:

> *"Haven't you read,"* He replied, *"that He who created[a] them in the beginning made them male and female,"* and He also said: *"For this reason, a man will leave his father and mother and be joined to his wife, and the two will become one flesh?"* (Matthew 19:4-5 HCSB)

As a result, we are shown clearly that Joseph and Mary had children after the virginal birth of Christ. As it is written: *"He is only the son of the carpenter. And his mother is Mary. His brothers are James, Joseph, Simon, and Judas. And all his sisters are here with us. So where does this man get all these things?"* (Matthew 13:55-56 ICB). This Scripture gives us the possibility that Joseph and Mary had, at least, a minimum of six children after the birth of Jesus Christ.

Of his sisters, we know nothing of certainty, but we do know that there were at least two of them. However, we do have Biblical evidence of two of his half-brothers and their roles in the Early Church. These two are James and Judah. We will start with James.

### James

Paul also makes mention of James as the brother of the Lord Jesus Christ in Galatians 1:19. *"... But I did not see any other* apostle except James, the Lord's brother..." (ISV). Likewise, in Galatians 2:9, Paul mentioned James as a pillar in the church:

> *When, therefore, James, Peter, and John (who were the recognised "pillars" of the church there) saw how God had given me his grace, they held out to Barnabas and me the right hand of fellowship, in full agreement that our mission was to the Gentiles and theirs to the Jews.* (PHILLIPS)

James, the half-brother of the Lord, received a personal visit from Christ shortly after His Resurrection.

> *... and that he appeared to Cephas and then to the twelve; after that, he appeared unto more than five hundred brothers at once, of whom the greater part remains unto now, but some are fallen asleep. After that, he appeared unto James; then to all the apostles.* (1 Corinthians 15:5-7 JUB)

We see here that Galatians 2:9 names James before it names Peter when it mentions the pillars of the church. With this, we can assume that James occupied a much more critical role of influence than did Peter. Also notable is the fact that Peter held high respect for James, to the point of almost having a fear of him. We can see this fear/respect relationship in Galatians 2:11-13:

*But when Peter was come to Antioch, I withstood him to the face, because he was to be blamed. For before that certain came from James, he did eat with the Gentiles: but when they were come, he withdrew and separated himself, fearing them which were of the circumcision. And the other Jews dissembled likewise with him; insomuch that Barnabas also was carried away with their dissimulation.* (KJV)

## James as an Apostol

This same James soon became a leader and one of the most influential figures in the Early Church in Jerusalem. We have seen in Galatians 1:19, that, by the time of this event, James was considered as one of the Apostles.

Similarly, we can see his authority and understood leadership in Acts 15:13. In this chapter, Simon testifies to how God used him to reach Cornelius and all those that were with him in his house for Christ. Peter did this even though Cornelius and his household were uncircumcised Gentiles. This act provoked the consternation of about all the leaders of the church in Jerusalem (Acts 10).

Notwithstanding, everybody was finally persuaded that the event was the work of God. They were convinced because of the clear evidence of the manifestation that these Gentiles had received the Baptism of the Holy Spirit with the evidence of speaking in tongues without having received previous instructions of the existence of such a blessing. Afterward, the Apostles

Paul and Joseph of Cyprus related what signs and wonders God had done through them among the Gentiles.

When they finished, James, the half-brother of the Lord Jesus Christ, took control of the council without anybody questioning his actions. *"And after they had held their peace, James answered, saying, Men and brethren, hearken unto me:"* (Acts 15:13 AKJV). When they continued, James gave a brief discourse and concluded by giving indications as to what the church should do. This verse is the first indication that James had entered the role of leadership among the Apostles and the church in Jerusalem.

It is essential that we notice that James passed over the testimonies of Paul and Joseph of Cyprus and went directly to the testimony of Simon Peter. We understand that they might have had several reasons for this action, but one of them was that Peter had much more authority and respect in the Jerusalem church than Paul enjoyed at that time.[45]

Nevertheless, how did James come to be counted as one of the twelve? To answer this question, we must remember that when Judas Iscariot died, the Apostles gathered to elect someone to take his place to complete the twelve (Acts 1:20-26).

By following the pattern and reasoning that they used in Acts 1:13-26, when Herod killed James the brother of John in Acts 12:2, it is a logical step to assume that they followed the same procedural outline to choose another. Because soon, we see James counted among their number. When Peter was miraculously delivered from the prison in the same chapter, we see Peter giving

---

[45] F.F. Bruce, *Commentary on the Book of the Acts, The New International Commentary on the New Testament*. Grand Rapids: Wm. B. Eerdmans Publishing Co., 1954.

account to James in Acts 12:17, "... *Tell this to James and the rest of the believers," he said; then he left and went somewhere else."*

James did not become a believer in the Divinity of his older brother until after the resurrection. It is evident that during the life and earthly ministry of Christ, he did not yet believe:

> *And he went home, and the crowd gathered again, so that they were not even able to eat a meal. And when his family heard this, they went out to restrain him, for they were saying, "He has lost his mind!"* (Mark 3:20-21 LEB)

> *... and Jesus' brothers urged him to go to Judea for the celebration. "Go where more people can see your miracles!" they scoffed. "You can't be famous when you hide like this! If you're so great, prove it to the world!" For even his brothers didn't believe in him.* (John 7:3-5 TLB)

In no way should we think that Jesus' half-brothers despised him. Instead, it was the age-old malady of simple sibling rivalry, just as all children and youth experience with their flesh and blood brothers and sisters even to this day. However, even though siblings enjoy poking and provoking one another when it comes to a real threat or danger to one of their own, pure love bursts forth. Because when one of them suffers serious harm, there are few that that love more, or suffer more than those same culprits, that are also their siblings, and that have been their micro-antagonists.

I believe that here, we find that James was profoundly moved when he saw his brother suffer and die in such a horrible manner. However, when Jesus appeared to him at His resurrection from the dead, the revelation was overwhelming, and the redemptive work of God was profoundly and brought to pass in his spirit and soul.

It is also true that James was the one person that had known Christ longer than any other among the twelve as-well-as being the only one that had known Christ his whole life. If we want to be accurate in our theology, soteriologically speaking, nobody was saved until after the resurrection of Christ, and it was precisely at the resurrection when James came to know Christ as his Savior. As I have stated, when he saw the resurrected Christ, his life was decisively transformed to make him the leader that he was born to be.

Finally, even though Mark is the first Gospel to be written, and it is the manuscript that many believe to have been the outline of the Synoptics, the epistle of James is the oldest book in the New Testament. Jacobs authority and patented leadership are clearly manifested by way of the impetus with which his book has been written. Some scholars affirm that there are more than fifty-five commands in its five short chapters.[46]

## Judah

Today, the name of Judas is as scorned as that of Hitler. When we hear this name, the first thing that comes to our minds is Judas

---

[46] C. Leslie Mitton, *The Epistle of James*, Eerdmans Press, Grand Rapids, MI 1966), p. 235, *This book mentions sixty instances example.*

Iscariot, he who betrayed our Lord. Because of this, the name is almost synonymous with treason. However, in the Bible, the name Judas was very common and appreciated. This stigma is another barrier that impedes a good understanding of the Scriptures for the lectors of our day; one of which protagonists of the first century did not have to contend. Therefore, we should remove the infamous disgrace from this name.

In Genesis 29:35, we find the first person known by this name in the Bible. We must to understand that Judas is merely the Greek word for (Ἰουδάς) Hebrew name Judah "*yehûdâh*" (יְהוּדָה), which means; Praise, or Praised be the Lord "*yâdâh*" (יְדָה).

Judas was such a common name that in the New Testament we could find at least six different people called Judas.[47] Among the six mentioned here, two of them are counted among the twelve Apostles: Judas, the *son* of James,[48] and Judas, *son* of Simon Iscariot.[49],[50]

In the same way, the book of the Bible that carries the name of Jude alludes directly to the fact that this is the Judas that is the

---

[47] (1) Judas Iscariot - Matthew 10:4; (2) Judas, Son of Joseph and Mary, the half-brother of the Lord – Matthew 13:55; (3) Judas, the son of James – Luke 6:16; (4) Judas of Galilee – Acts 5:37; (5) Judas of Damascus – Acts 9:11; (6) Judas, also called Barsabbas – Acts 15:22.

[48] Luke 6:16; John 14:22; Acts 1:13.

[49] John 6:71; "*Y hablaba de Judas Iscariote, hijo de Simón, porque éste era el que le iba a entregar, y era uno de los doce.*"

[50] "*Easton's Bible Dictionary: New and revised ed.*" published by T. Nelson and Sons. The name "Iscariot" is the Hebrew demonym meaning: "Originally from Kerioth." Kerioth was the name of two cities in the Bible. It is mentioned in Amos 2:2, "*So I will send a fire upon Moab, and it shall devour the strongholds of Kerioth, and Moab shall die amid uproar, amid shouting and the sound of the trumpet.*" (KJV). It is also mentioned in Jeremiah 48:24, "*and Kerioth, and Bozrah, and all the cities of the land of Moab, far and near.*" (KJV).

son of Joseph and Mary, and the brother of James.[51] This same Judas identifies himself as the brother of James, who in turn, identified himself as the half-brother of the Lord.[52]

In support of James' authority as mentioned earlier, the only reason for him to mention him in the book of Jude is that this James is Jude's brother. This James is the same person that is widely known as the leader in the church of his day. As we have seen, James, the half-brother of the Lord, was the only person with this name that held such full recognition. James the brother of John, though he was one of the original Apostles, never obtained the same notoriety in the church. Thus, we can see that this Judas is the same that is mentioned in Matthew 13:55. Nonetheless, he did not even feel worthy to identify himself as the half-brother of the Lord. He called himself, *"a servant of Jesus Christ"* (Jude 1)

Therefore, we can conclude that James and this Judas are among those that Paul counted with those that were called the brothers of the Lord in 1st Corinthians 9:5. With this, we can also deduce that these two leaders of the church and ministers of the Gospel, were married men. *"Do we not have the right to take along a believing wife as do other apostles, the brothers of the Lord, and Cephas?"* (MEV).

---

[51] R.V. Tasker. *The Gospel according to Saint Matthew.* InterVarsity Press. 1961. p. 36

[52] Galatians 1:19

# Chapter 4

# EXAMPLES OF UNRECOGNIZED FAMILIES

To give an example of the Catholic influence I have been referencing, I would like to bring out a known passage and a concept that has been present along with it that we have readily accepted.

### The Road to Emmaus

I believe that we have all seen this famous painting titled, *The Road to Emmaus*. In this work of art two men are pictured walking back home after the resurrection of our Lord. We also see Christ there speaking with them. This painting is a representation of an event that happened in Luke 24:13-35, and it is a beautiful testimony.

It has always seemed entirely reasonable and unquestionable to imagine it in this way; that is, for it to have been 'two men' walking on the road to Emmaus. However, according to what the Bible indicates, this is not what we should conclude from this account from Luke's Gospel.

In the manifestation of the resurrected Christ on the road to Emmaus, apart from Jesus, one other person is identified by name. Luke 24:18 says: "*One of them, Cleopas,[53] replied, "Are you the only one in Jerusalem who doesn't know what has happened recently?"* (NOG).

A valid question that we could ask about this might be: "*Why is it that of all the people that Christ could have chosen to have manifested Himself in his glorified resurrected state on this first day, that He chose these two?*" The answer is simple, but the key is found in the Gospel of John 19:25 that says: "*Standing by the cross of Jesus were his mother and his mother's sister, Mary the wife of Clopas, and Mary of Magdala...*" (NABRE).

I want to point something out here. In Luke, on the morning of the resurrection, we find Cleopas returning to his home from Jerusalem. John says that his wife was in Jerusalem at the foot of the cross when Jesus died. It is evident in the narrations of all the evangelists that there was no time to leave Jerusalem after the death and burial of Christ because the Sabbath was fast approaching. Nevertheless, we see Cleopas returning home from Jerusalem the morning after the Sabbath, that is, the morning of the resurrection, but somebody else was with him. I do believe that we can safely assume that the other person that is with him is his wife, Mary.

## Mary, Mary, Mary

Also, it is a debate as to if there are three or four women mentioned in John 19:25. What might present a confusion for some that conclude that there are four women here, is

---

[53] Κλεόπας

something quite simple. We are talking about the literary style of identification that is employed. The author is using the same style of expression of identification used when a family member is of somebody that is introduced, and either one or the other is more known to the receptors of the writing. For example:

- "... *and John the brother of James, ...*" (Mark 3:17; see also 5:37; and Acts 12:2)
- "... *Judas the brother of James...*" (Luke 6:16; see also Acts 1:13)
- "... *Andrew, Simon Peter's brother, ...*" (John 1:40; see also 6:8)
- "*Jude, the servant of Jesus Christ, and brother of James, ...*" (Jude 1:1).

With the application of this simple rule of literary style, we have a harmony with the other two Synoptics that inform us that there were three women and not four at the foot of the cross. Therefore, we read these two phrases as one thought when it says: "*... and his mother's sister, Mary, the wife of Clopas...*" That is to say that Mary, the mother of Jesus, had a sister also named Mary, who was the wife of Cleopas.

In Mark 15:40 we find a parallel passage that names three women that witnessed the crucifixion of Christ. "*There were also some women looking on from a distance, among whom were*

*Mary Magdalene, and Mary the mother of James the Less and Joses, and Salome...."* (NASB)[54]

We also have Matthew 27:56 as a parallel verse: *"Mary Magdalene, and Mary the mother of James and Joseph, and the mother of James and John were there..."* (NCV). It becomes even more interesting when we read this same verse in another translation: *"Mary Magdalene was among them. Mary, the mother of James and Joseph, was also there. So was the mother of Zebedee's sons..."* (NIRV).

Here we have three testimonies that say the same things, but that hold the appearance of presenting discrepancies; that is until you study them with a tad bit more attention. Now then, one thing that we see in common is that all of them say that there are three women present. The evangelists have identified one of these three women without leaving us any doubt, and that is Mary Magdalene. However, the apparent difference is found in the identity of the other two women. We should ask the question as to why.

Matthew 27:55 makes us think even more. It says: *"Many women who had followed Jesus from Galilee and given him support were also there, watching from a distance..."* (NET). Even though this verse makes it clear that there were other women present, these authors felt the obligation to explicitly set three apart from the rest of them. We are forced to decide if this decision was random, or if the identity of these women was

---

[54] In Greek "I⌀ωσή" (José – Josef – Joseph). It is also necessary to observe Mark 15:47 *"Mary Magdalene and Mary the mother of Joseph were watching and saw where the body of Jesus was placed."* Also compare Matthew 27:56 *"Among them were Mary Magdalene, Mary the mother of James and Joseph, and the wife of Zebedee."*

intentional and particularly relevant to the original recipients of these Gospels.

In Matthew, we have *"Mary Magdalene, and Mary, the mother of James and Joseph, and Mary, mother of Zebedee's sons..."* (James and John). In Mark, we have *"Mary Magdalene, Mary the mother of James the lesser, and Joseph, and Salome."* Finally, in John 19:25 we have *"... his mother and his mother's sister, Mary the wife of Clopas, and Mary of Magdala."*

I propose that the naming of these women is profoundly intentional and that the three authors are talking about the same three women. However, I believe that the authors were presenting them in the way that they would be recognized and identified more readily by the initially intended audience that received that specific Gospel from the said author.

Therefore, this leads us to understand that Mary Magdalene was identified in this manner almost universally. Given that we find so many "Marys" in the New Testament, I also maintain that this Mary Magdalene is the same Mary that is identified as the sister of Martha in Luke 10:38-42; and the sister of Lazarus in John11:1-44. Furthermore, I believe that she is the woman described in Luke 7:38-46, and in John12:3.

These two verses say:

> *And behold, a woman in the city who was a sinner, when she knew that Jesus sat at the table in the Pharisee's house, brought an alabaster flask of fragrant oil, 38 and stood at His feet behind Him weeping; and she began to wash His feet with her tears, and wiped them with the hair of her head;*

*and she kissed His feet and anointed them with the fragrant oil. 39 Now when the Pharisee who had invited Him saw this, he spoke to himself, saying, "This Man, if He were a prophet, would know who and what manner of woman this is who is touching Him, for she is a sinner."*

*And Jesus answered and said to him, "Simon, I have something to say to you."*

*So, he said, "Teacher, say it."*

*"There was a certain creditor who had two debtors. One owed five hundred denarii, and the other fifty. 42 And when they had nothing with which to repay, he freely forgave them both. Tell Me, therefore, which of them will love him more?"*

*Simon answered and said, "I suppose the one whom he forgave more."*

*And He said to him, "You have rightly judged." 44 Then He turned to the woman and said to Simon, "Do you see this woman? I entered your house; you gave Me no water for My feet, but she has washed My feet with her tears and wiped them with the hair of her head. 45 You gave Me no kiss, but this woman has not ceased to kiss My feet since the time I came in. 46 You did not anoint My head with oil, but this woman has anointed My feet with fragrant oil...* (Luke 7:37-46 NKJV).

*Then Mary took about a pint of pure nard, an expensive perfume; she poured it on Jesus' feet and wiped his feet with her hair. And the house was filled with the fragrance of the perfume...."* (John12:3 NIV).

## Diverse Languages

The main problem we find consists in understanding or considering the cultural aspects of the names in the different languages that were in everyday use in the region in the first century. We also must contemplate the influence of the Greek and Latin translations of these names.

In Matthew and Mark, the mother of James the Lesser and Joseph is Mary the mother of Jesus, as identified in John 19:25. Without a doubt, the Gospels in Mark 6:3 and Matthew 13:55-56 testify that James and Joseph were the half-brothers of Jesus. James was the first that was born after Christ, and the first-born of Joseph the Carpenter. Joseph is the second born son of Joseph and Mary and was born after James.

> (Mark 6:3 NLT) *Then they scoffed, "He's just a carpenter, the son of Mary[a] and the brother of James, Joseph, Judas, and Simon. And his sisters live right here among us." They were deeply offended and refused to believe in him.*

> (Matthew 13:55-56 NIVUK) *'Isn't this the carpenter's son? Isn't his mother's name Mary, and aren't his brothers James, Joseph, Simon, and Judas? 56 Aren't all his sisters with us? Where then did this man get all these things?'*

We can deduce that the reason that the James mentioned in Mark 15:40 is called James the Less, Lesser, or Younger (ιακωβου του μικρου),[55] (depending on your English translation), was so that he not be confused with James, the older brother of John and the son of Zebedee. It can easily be assumed that James, the older brother of John was also older than James, the half-brother of Jesus Christ. In a tad bit, we shall speak of this in more detail.

What is it that we know of Salome? We know that she has been referred to as Mary Salome, and this might answer some of our questions. Mary is her Latin name, and Salome or *"Shelomah"* (שלומית) is her Hebrew name. It is a name that comes from the Hebrew word "Shalom," or "Peace" (שלום).

*Easton's Bible Dictionary* says of her:

> *The wife of Zebedee and mother of James and John (Mat 27:56), and probably the sister of Mary, the mother of our Lord (John 19:25). She sought for her son's places of honor in Christ's kingdom (Matthew 20:20 Matthew 20:21; comp 19:28). She witnessed the crucifixion (Mark 15:40) and was*

---

[55] Greek Old Testament (Greek OT), Deutsche Bibelgesellschaft, Balinger Straße 31A 70567 Stuttgart Germany. Revised ed. edition (March 9, 2007).

*present with the other women at the sepulcher (Matthew 27:56).*[56]

In the same way, *Smith's Bible Dictionary* agrees with this identity of Salome as the sister of Mary, the mother of Jesus Christ.[57]

I am also in agreement, and with this, I settle that John 19:25 is talking about three women and not four. Furthermore, if we read in this context, we have all the names of the women at the foot of the cross in all the Gospels. This is exegetical harmony and a faithful congruence of the Gospels. Nobody is unidentified, and this is the idea and purpose of the author in this verse. However, we still have questions to answer. The next question is, "Who, then, is Cleopas?"

To fully answer this, we must investigate two other questions concerning Cleopas and this verse. As I have said, the first is, "Who is He?" The second question is, "Who are all the "Marys" in this passage?

> (1) Some translations make a distinction of names when mentioning this protagonist in Luke and John. This dissimilarity provokes a doubt as to if we are talking about one person or two different people. These translations use the name "Cleopas" in Luke and the name of "Clopas" in John.

---

[56] M.G. Easton, *Easton's Bible Dictionary*, Salome. T. Nelson and Sons, London, Edinburgh, and New York. 1894. Christiananswers.net, https://christiananswers.net/dictionary/salome.html (accessed April 21, 2019).

[57] William Smith, *Smith's Bible Dictionary*, Salome. John Murray Publishers, London, 1863.

(2) How are we going to have two sisters named Mary? (John 19:25)

Richard R. Losch claims that the name Clopas in John 19:25 ("*Mary the wife of Clopas*" Κλωπᾶς) is the Greek form of the Aramaic "Klofa o Qlofa" (קלופא), and the name Cleopas (Κλεόπας) is the abbreviated form of the name "Cleopatros", a Greek name that means "The Glory of the Father". (Its feminine form Cleopatra is better known).[58] I agree with Losch's assertion, for I also believe that we are indeed referring to the same person in two different languages.

Nevertheless, historically, we have Papias, Hegesippus, the second-century church chronicler, and Eusebius of Caesarea also from the second century that confess the same argument that I present in this discourse. They believed that Cleopas was the brother of Joseph, the husband of Mary, the mother of Jesus. Eusebius of Caesarea spoke of this in his writings, "The History of the Church" (Book III, Chapter 11).[59]

Now then, in the Western mentality, it might strike some as a bit strange, but not unheard of, that two brothers from one

---

[58] Richard R. Losch. *All the people in the Bible: An A-Z guide to the saints*, William B. Eerdsmans Publications, 2140 Oak Industrial Drive, N.E., Grand Rapids, Michigan, 49505. 2008 (Page 279)

[59] Eusebius of Caesarea, Church History, Book III, Chapter 11. "*How Simeon led the church in Jerusalem after James – (XI) After the martyrdom of James and the immediate taking of Jerusalem, a tradition is told that, coming from different places, they gathered in one place the apostles and the disciples of the Lord that were still found alive, and together with them also were those of the Lord's family according to the flesh (because many of them were still alive). All of them deliberated about who should be judged worthy to take James' place, and unanimously all agreed that Simeon, the son of Clofas (who also is mentioned in the text of the Gospel), was worthy of the throne in that region, because he was, according to as they said, the cousin of the Savio, because Hegesipo tells us that Clofas was Joseph's brother.*"

family would marry two sisters from another. (On a personal level, I have two sisters-in-law that have married two brothers from another family.)

Even still, in the Middle and the Far East, it would have been reasonable for a family to agree to a marriage covenant with the son of one family and the daughter of another. However, if the families found it to be an appropriate arrangement, and if both families were in consensus, it would not have been atypical to convene another marriage covenant for another one of their sons or daughters.

This brings up another question if Easton and Smith are correct, and I think that they are. However, if Mary Salome is the wife of Zebedee, how is she then the wife of Cleopas? Also, we must ask, if Zebedee was a prosperous fisher from the region of Galilee, how did he come to own a home in Judea near the city of Jerusalem?

Now we have two more questions, but this is a good thing because we are here to learn. So, we should take the time to examine the historical, socio-cultural, geographical, and geopolitical situations of this region in the first century and answer these inquiries. In this way, we can have a point of reference to answer questions that we still have to face to have a clear understanding of the world in which John Mark lived, and the people that surrounded him in his environment.

### Cleopas y Zebedee

The name Zebedee is mentioned twelve times in the New Testament. It is mentioned six times in Matthew; Four times in

Mark; once in Luke; and once in John. I have indicated that Cleopas is a Greek name. Nevertheless, just like almost all the characters to whom we are presented in the New Testament, Cleopas had a Greek or a Latin name, as well as a Hebrew name, and his Hebrew name was Zebedee. Zebedee is the Greek pronunciation of his Hebrew name "*Zabdi*" (זבדי), which means, "Gifted, or Generous Giver".

As I have indicated and will continue to point out, it was not unusual for people of that region in the first century to have two names in two different languages. Cleopas and Zebedee are the same people recognized by two different names in two different languages.

### A Fisherman from Galilee with a House the Judea

The fall of the Kingdom of Judah and the Babylonian captivity brought total repentance to the people. When they were repatriated to their inheritances, we can see in the books of Nehemiah and Ezra how they established themselves to affirm their faith and fidelity to the Lord.

We learn that Ezra established the *Sopherim*. They were the early scribes that reproduced the copies of the Torah, The Prophets, and the Writings by hand for every one of the communities in which a population of Jews lived. In this way, they could gather faithfully every Sabbath day to study, meditate, and learn from the Law of the Lord.

After them, came the Masoretes, or better known as the doctors of the Law. Their disciples were the rabbis that were trained and were sent to live in almost every city and village, even in the diaspora, where ten or more Jewish men lived. If they found ten or more Jewish men, they would start a synagogue. In every synagogue, they studied the copies of the Scriptures made by the Sopherim.

Part of their repentance and reconciliation with the Lord was to keep the Holy Convocations, beginning with their faithfulness to the Sabbath. Also included was their attendance of the seven holy feast days, as much as was within their power to do so, from where ever they lived. The two most popular ones were the Passover and the Feast of Tabernacles.

Now then, because of these holy feast days, almost all the Jews kept one, or more inheritances for their families in Judea, even though they lived in some distant part of the Roman Empire because of the diaspora. Others, being that they had to go up to Jerusalem periodically, bought property so that they, or that members of their families could lodge there when they had to go up to the Holy City. It would not have made sense to have to struggle to look for lodging every time you had to go, knowing that you, or somebody in your family would eventually have to go up to Jerusalem.

Therefore, even though Zebedee was a fisher from Galilee, he owned property near Jerusalem to house his family when they went up to the feast days in Judea. We shall be seeing other examples of this in the trajectory of this discourse.

This done for the moment, let us move on to more details concerning the many *"Marys"* that we see in Scripture.

## Mara, Mary, Miriam, Maryam, Mirjam

Although we have addressed this idea partially, and indirectly, it is now time to deal with the second question of this point: How can we have, what appears to be two sisters with the same name? First, we have mentioned the fact that Mary, the sister of the mother of our Lord was also known as Salome.

However, there is a cultural motive that is even more informative, and that is indispensable to understand this regional first-century custom. As I have previously alluded, what we must contemplate when we address this subject are the socio-historical, geographical, and geopolitical backgrounds of the people and regions of the people of which we wish to investigate.

Before I enter the elemental concept of this part of my argument, I want to give an example from the Old Testament of a family that gave similar names to their sons. I am referring to the case of Johanan (*Jehovah has favored*) and Jonathan (*Jehovah has Given*), the sons of Kareah in Jeremiah 40:8. Some English translations have done a poor job of translating this verse. These versions only name one of the sons of Kareah, I believe, because they are so similar, even in the Hebrew, but they are even more similar when translated into English.

For many of the 21st-century Western culture, unless the children are twins, it seems unreasonable or incomprehensible to give your children the same name or such similar sounding names. However, it was not like that with the Hebrews. They did not seek so much the beauty of the sound of the name that they wanted to give to their children, but the significance of the name. There are cases in which the names are completely different, but the significance is entirely synonymous. Nevertheless, in other instances, we have names that sound very much alike, but the significance is entirely different.

## Originally, What Did It Mean to Be a Jew?

In the context of our cases of names simply being translated as Mary, we are talking about Jewish families that came into a region that, historically, did not pertain to the Jews, but the Samaritans. When I say Samaritans, I am referring to the fact that it belonged to the descendants of the Kingdom of Israel of the Old Testament. In this section, I will give a brief explanation of the historical background of this region, the tribal affiliations, and the why and how we find the situation that we see in the New Testament.

The word "Jew" is the indication that someone was a descendant of the Kingdom of Judah. Even a casual study of the Scriptures will show you that the word "Jew" does not appear in the Bible until the book of Esther, in Esther 2:5: *"Now there was a Jew in the citadel of Susa whose name was Mordecai son of Jair son of Shimei son of Kish, a Benjaminite..."* (NRSV).

The reason for this is because, in the Babylonian captivity, the only ones that were taken there were from the Kingdom of Judah. All of them were Jews in the sense of the place of their origin; it was their demonym. This means that of the twelve tribes of Israel, only three were citizens of the Kingdom of Judah:

- The tribe of Judah,
- The tribe of Levi, and

- The tribe of Benjamin.

For the Benefit and the edification of those that, perhaps, have not contemplated this perspective, or previously understood this fact, I will continue further with the following contextual and historical explanation.

We know that there were only twelve tribes of Israel. However, we read in 1st Kings 11:30-32 that when Jeroboam encountered the prophet Ahijah, the prophet took off the new garment that he had and tore it into twelve pieces. Then, the prophet said something, that for us, frequently goes unnoticed, or, is misinterpreted.

> *when Ahijah laid hold of the new garment, he was wearing and tore it into twelve pieces. He then said to Jeroboam: Take for yourself ten pieces; for thus says the Lord, the God of Israel, 'See, I am about to tear the kingdom from the hand of Solomon and will give you ten tribes. One tribe will remain his, for the sake of my servant David and for the sake of Jerusalem, the city that I have chosen out of all the tribes of Israel...* (1st Kings 11:30-32 NRSVA)

The detail that we should pay attention to is this. When we count the twelve tribes of Israel, we never count the tribe of Joseph. Depending on the English translation, the tribe of Joseph is only mentioned, outright, twice in the Bible; in Numbers 13:11, and in Revelations 7:8. You might find that in certain translations, the tribe of Joseph is mentioned on several occasions. However, more accurately these are references to the origins of the tribes of Manasseh and Efraim.

Therefore, in the Old Testament, instead of mentioning the tribe of Joseph, it always mentions Joseph's two sons, Manasseh and Efraim. The reason for this is that, when Joseph presented his two sons to his father, Jacob proclaimed that Joseph's sons were now his. *"Therefore, your two sons, who were born to you in the land of Egypt before I came to you in Egypt, are now mine; Ephraim and Manasseh shall be mine, just as Reuben and Simeon are..."* (Genesis 48:5 NRSVACE).

In this way, Jacob gave Joseph the firstborn's share and doubled his inheritance, because both of his sons received their inheritance as an independent tribe. This fact demands our attention because the key word in this entire matter is the word "inheritance." Nevertheless, we see clearly in the Scriptures that the tribe of Levi did not receive an inheritance in the Promised Land. *"Therefore, Levi has no allotment or inheritance with his kindred; the Lord is his inheritance, as the Lord your God promised him..."* (Deuteronomy 10:9 NRSVCE).[60]

Even still, in the division of the Kingdom, we see that the tribe of Benjamin remained faithful to the house of David.

> *When Rehobo'am came to Jerusalem, he assembled all the house of Judah, and the tribe of Benjamin, a hundred and eighty thousand chosen warriors, to fight against the house of Israel, to*

---

[60] See also Numbers 18:21, Deuteronomy 10:9; 18:1, and Joshua 13:14, 33.

> *restore the kingdom to Rehobo'am, the son of Solomon...* (1 Kings 12:21 RSV)

When the prophet Ahijah said to Solomon: *"One tribe will remain his, for the sake of my servant David and for the sake of Jerusalem..."*, he was referring to the tribe of Benjamin because without a doubt, the tribe of Judah was going to stay faithful to the house of David being that the King's Household was of this tribe.

We know that when Jeroboam succeeded in dividing the kingdom, he abandoned the worship of the Lord God to invent his own religion. This he did to keep the people from going up to worship in Jerusalem, and thus exposing themselves to be convinced by Rehoboam to return to him. The tribe of Levi, seeing that they had no inheritance, nor work in the Northern Kingdom, emigrated to the Southern Kingdom from all of their cities that the other tribes had loaned to them, to continue in their positions and obligations In the Temple in Jerusalem.

Being that Levi had no inheritance, and the tribe of Joseph was, in reality, the tribes of Manasseh and Efraim, with these last two, you have the ten tribes of the Northern Kingdom. However, the truth is that we should not see it as if Jeroboam had ten tribes, but rather, that he had the wealth of these ten tribes at his disposition. By comparison and according to a mere human and materialistic perspective, the Kingdom of Israel was much wealthier than the Kingdom of Judah.

The Kingdom of the North had the Lake of Galilee, the Jordan River, numerous fountains of water and creeks, fertile lands, and an abundance of green forests. Meanwhile, by comparison, the only great body of water that the Southern Kingdom had was the Dead Sea. The mountainous area around Jerusalem was green and well-watered and ideal for raising sheep and other livestock and had many beautiful cities and settlements. Nevertheless, the rest of the region was what we could confidently say was like a desolate desert.

As concerning the tribes and inheritances of the Kingdom of Judah that would remain with David; we have Benjamin, the tribe mentioned by Ahijah. Remember, the tribe of Levi did not have an inheritance to contribute to the material wealth of the kingdom. In fact, in the material and carnal sense, the tribe of Levi could have been considered a liability and a burden instead of a people that contributed to the riches and prosperity of the nation.

Before the division of the kingdom, the twelve tribes (remember Ephraim and Manasseh) contributed to the support and well-being of the tribe of Levi. Now, all the responsibility rested firmly on the shoulders of just two tribes because the Law of the Lord decreed that the other tribes had the responsibility to support the Levites financially and materially.

With this economic support, the Levites could dedicate themselves entirely to their obligations in the service of the Lord in the Temple. Above all else, this tribe had the Lord Himself as their inheritance. The dedicated service of the Levites, in turn, contributed the blessing of the spiritual life and the favor of the Lord over the people, which added up to the prosperity of the entire Kingdom. This was the primary reason that the Kingdom of Judah survived for almost two-hundred years more than the Kingdom of Israel.

We can see how Nehemiah, from his perspective after the Babylonian captivity, deemed the lack of economic support of the Levites as a genuine threat to the security of the kingdom in Nehemiah 13:10-12:

> *I also learned that the portions for the Levites had not been provided and that each of the Levites and singers who performed the work had gone back to his own field. So, I rebuked the leaders and asked, "Why has the House of God been forsaken?" I assembled them and stationed them at their posts. Then all Judah brought the tithe of grain, new wine, and oil to the storehouses.* (Nehemiah 13:10-12 TLV)

In the post-captivity books of Ezra and Nehemiah, the Levites fulfilled a crucial role, because they helped Ezra to teach the Law of the Lord.[61] As a result of their service and diligence, we can see Judaism at its zenith of development to receive the Messiah in the days of the New Testament. Therefore, in the New Testament, we have the Levites always mentioned as Jews. We also have Zacharias and Elisabeth, the parents of John the

---

[61] (2 Chronicles 35:3) *"He said to the Levites who taught all Israel and who were consecrated to Adonai, "Put the holy Ark in the House which Solomon the son of King David of Israel built. Since it is no longer a burden on your shoulders now, serve Adonai your God and His people Israel."* This verse does not take place during the days of Ezra, but it demonstrates the role of the Levites teaching the people during the days of the reformations of King Josiah.

We also have the example of Nehemiah 8:9 *"When the people heard what the Law required; they were so moved that they began to cry. So Nehemiah, who was the governor, Ezra, the priest and scholar of the Law, and the Levites who were explaining the Law told all the people, "This day is holy to the LORD your God, so you are not to mourn or cry."*

Baptist, the second cousin of the Lord, as an example and evidence of Levites as Jews.[62] Finally, we cannot forget the Apostle Paul, a Jew from the tribe of Benjamin (Romans 11:1) (Philippians 3:4-5).

Therefore, we can see that the Kingdom of the North or the Samaritans were the ten tribes of the Kingdom of Israel, and the Kingdom of Judah were primarily the three tribes to the south.

**Ethiopian Jews**

Now then, with what I have explained thus far, it is inevitable to ask the question about the existence of the Ethiopian Jews. With them, we have a whole different case study, but it is easily explained. They are known today in Israel as the Falasha; which means, foreigners or exiled ones, even though they much prefer to be called Beta Israel.[63]

There are two fundamental theories as to their origin:

1.) The Beta Israelis claim that they are the descendants of the son of King Solomon, and the queen of Sheba after her visit to the great king of Israel in 1 Kings 10:1-13.

This theory is a large, but not unheard-of part of the Ethiopian tradition. The great royal shield of the imperial house of Ethiopia says that it is "The House of Solomon" (The House

---

[62] Luke 1:5-38

[63] M'Sur. Falasha. https://msur.es/religiones/judaismo/falasha/. (Accessed 02/11/2019)

of David). The name of the last king was, *Ras Tafari Makonnen Woldemikael*[64],[65] (known in the Western world by his throne name as, "*Haile Selassie*." This reign was of such greatness that the country of Ethiopia is the only African country that was never under the dominion of European colonization.

In his genealogy, they announce in agreement with the confession of the Falasha, that he is a direct descendant of King Solomon and the queen of Sheba[66] and their son Menelik I (which means the son of the wise one). Counting from Menelik I to Haile Selassie, there were two hundred and twenty-five generations.[67] The official history of the nation informs us that Haile Selassie is the last member of the Solomonic Dynasty, that traced his lineage back to the Emperor Menelik 1, according to the ancestral registry.

Although it is believed that the Solomonic Dynasty was the stronghold of Judaism, and afterward of Ethiopian Orthodox Christianity with its reign since the 10th century B.C.,[68] outside of the Ethiopian affirmations, and though it is not improbable,

---

[64] Haggai Erlich, *The Cross and the River: Ethiopia, Egypt, and the Nile.* (2002) Lynne Rienner Publishers, Boulder, Colorado, USA. p. 192. "

[65] The Rastafari (followers of de Ras Tafari) have existed since the Emperor Ras Tafari Makonnen was crowned in 1930. His title was "*His Majesty Imperial Haile Selassie I, the Conqueror and Lion of the Tribe of Judah, King of Kings of Ethiopia and Chosen by God.*"

[66] Haile Selassie Biography | Birthday, Trivia | Ethiopian, https://www.who2.com/bio/haile-selassie/ (accessed April 22, 2019).

[67] "*Solomonid Dynasty - Ethiopian history*". britannica.com. https://www.britannica.com/search?query=Solomonid+dynasty+%28Ethiopian+history%29. (accessed 02/10/2019).

[68] Getatchew Haile, " *The Ethiopian Orthodox Church's Tradition on the Holy Cross.* Brill, Leiden, Netherlands, 2017.

we have to say that there is little evidence historical evidence of this supposition.

Another interesting point in this conversation is about the Ark of the Covenant that was in the Temple in Jerusalem. At some point in time, the Ark disappeared from Jerusalem. The Scriptures leave a blank space as per what happened to it after the fall of Jerusalem to the Babylonians. There is no lack of theories as to its whereabouts. One viable theory is a tunnel that was found under the city of Jerusalem that a colleague of mine, the distinguished archaeologist, Dr. Scott Stripling, is investigating.[69]

Another supposition as to the resting place of the Ark of the Covenant is that seeing the imminent attack and conquest of Jerusalem by Nebuchadnezzar's army, the Ark was transported to Ethiopia and hidden there under the security of faithful Jews. Many have attempted to prove this theory with substantial evidence that would verify this possibility. Among them was the renowned archaeologist, Dr. Stuart C. Munro-Hay. To investigate this possibility, he explored and wrote a book of this contingency called, *Aksum: An African Civilisation of Late Antiquity*.[70]

I conclude this point by saying that these origins are a position that they uphold. Nevertheless, I must add a note here just for information's sake: The followers of King Haile Selassie known as the Ras Tafari. "Ras," the first part of his name means "prince, head, and respected leader," and Tafarí, the second

---

[69] Ari Feldman, *Archaeologists Hunt for Ark of The Covenant in Israel*. July 17, 2017. Read more: https://forward.com/fast-forward/377171/watch-archaeologists-hunt-for-ark-of-the-covenant-in-israel/. Accessed 02/03/2019.

[70] Stuart C. Munro-Hay, *Aksum: An African Civilisation of Late Antiquity*, Edinburgh University Press, 1991,

name of Emperor Haile Selassie, in the Amharic, which is Ethiopia's Semitic language. Taking the title of Rastafari is a confession that a person is a follower of Tafari *Makonnen*, even though he vehemently denied being some a kind of messiah because he confessed to being a Christian and a follower of Jesus Christ.

2.) The second and the more coherent theory on the origin of the Ethiopian Jews is found in the book of Esther. Esther 1:1 says that: "... *Now it came to pass in the days of Ahasuerus - this is Ahasuerus who reigned, from India even unto Ethiopia, over a hundred and seven and twenty provinces*" (JPS). However, in Esther 8:17, it says:

*And in every province, and in every city, whithersoever the king's commandment and his decree came, the Jews had gladness and joy, a feast, and a good day. And many from among the peoples of the land became Jews; for the fear of the Jews was fallen upon them.* (Esther 8:17).

Keep in mind that the book of Esther is about the Judean captivity and that Hadasa and Mordecai were of the tribe of Benjamin (Esther 2:6-7).

First, we must concede to the fact that there were Jews in Ethiopia before this great movement of proselytism found in the book of Esther took place. There had to be Jews there for the proselytes to know what a Jew was so that they might convert to Judaism. Though there are other postulations, this fact could give some credence to the prior theories that have been presented. These first Jews, whoever they were, and their proselytes were the progenitors of all the thousands of the Ethiopian Jews that we find in Israel to this day.

Consequently, we find the Ethiopian eunuch, a man of high authority under Candace the queen of the Ethiopians, in the book of Acts 8:26-40 that had gone up to worship in Jerusalem. This man was not a Gentile or a God-Fearer as some suppose, but he was a naturally born Jew, and his family had probably been Jewish for at least Thirteen generations according to Matthew 1:17.

**Jews in the Northern Kingdom**

Even still, as we learn in 2nd Chronicles 30, there was a time of mercy and the last call of repentance to the Kingdom of Israel during the reformations of King Hezekiah. This call to repentance and reformation is the only reason that we find specific individuals in the New Testament with the demonym of Jews that were descendants of tribes whose inheritances were initially found in the Northern Kingdom, and not in the Kingdom of Judah. They were from the tribes of Asher, Manasseh, and of Zebulun.[71]

---

[71] 2nd Chronicles 30:10-11 (VOICE) *"When the messengers took this message throughout the Northern Kingdom, most of the Northerners ridiculed and ignored the message. But some people from the Northern tribes of Asher, Manasseh, and Zebulun obeyed Hezekiah and the leaders and humbly traveled to Jerusalem just as all of the Southern Kingdom were given one mind and obeyed under the guidance of the True God via the command of the king and his officials."*

For this reason, we find that the prophetess Anna, the daughter of Phanuel, was Jewish, even though she was from the tribe of Asher. (Luke 2:36) *"There was also a prophetess called Anna, the daughter of Phanuel, of the tribe of Asher. She was of a great age, having been widowed after a seven-year marriage..."* (NTE).

It is indispensable that we keep in mind that with the added exceptions of the Ethiopians, and the individuals that left their inheritances to return to Jerusalem to worship the Lord and not Jeroboam's foreign gods, all the Jews were from the tribes of Judah, Benjamin, and Levi.

During the time of the Northern Kingdom, the most powerful and influential king was Omri. In the seventh year of his reign, he bought the hill of Samaria from Shemer for two talents of silver, and he fortified it. He also built his palace there.[72] Omri called the name of the city that he built Samaria, after the name of Shemer, the former owner of the hill. (1 Kings 16:24). Therefore, the capital city of the Northern Kingdom changed from the city of Tirzah to Samaria, and that is where it remained.

Consequently, in the New Testament, the survivors of the Northern Kingdom, the descendants of the sons of Jacob of the Kingdom of Israel, we know only as the Samaritans. The term "Samaritan" was the demonym that indicated Samaria, the capital city of the Northern Kingdom before its fall. They were

---

[72] *Author's Note: I have been to the archeological dig site of the remains of this palace. It was begun by a team from Harvard University during the 1908 until the 1930s but had to end because events that led up to WWII. It is in Palestinian territory. The location and the ruins of the palace are so beautiful that much later King Herod the Great built a palace about three hundred meters from the site, and there are numerous Roman ruins there as well. There is an amphitheater and the ruins of a Roman settlement there as well.*

children of Israel but were not Jews. Nevertheless, they were inheritors of the promise of the Messiah. This is why Christ presented Himself and preached to them.[73]

Nazareth and the whole region of Lake Kinnereth[74] did not belong to the Kingdom of Judah, but of the Kingdom of Israel. When the Northern Kingdom fell to the Assyrians in the years 721-22 B.C., they deported most of the people and began to fill the land promised to the Children of Israel with people of other nations.

> *The king of Assyria brought men from Babylon, from Cuthah, from Avva, and from Hamath and Sepharvaim, and placed them in the cities of Samaria instead of the children of Israel; and they possessed Samaria and lived in its cities.* (2 Kings 17:24 WEB)

However, we must keep in mind that not all the inhabitants of the Kingdom of Israel were permanently deported (2 Kings 17:24-34). Many of them were explicitly repatriated to teach the people that the King of Assyria had sent to occupy the land how to worship their god. Remember, the Kingdom of Israel

---

[73] John 4:4-40

[74] National Oceanic and Atmospheric Administration, *"What's the difference between an ocean and a sea?"* https://oceanservice.noaa.gov/facts/oceanorsea.html. *Lake Kinneret(th), or Genezaret(th) is actually the correct, or more technical and geologically correct term for the "Sea of Galilee." In terms of geography, a sea is found on the margins of the ocean and are partially enclosed by land. A sea is always connected to an ocean. If it is completely enclosed by land it is geologically classified as a lake. Seas. Seas are smaller than oceans and are usually located where the land and ocean meet.*

never fully reconciled with God, so their worship was an abominable hybrid of the worship of Jehovah and pagan practices. These ethnic groups did not just disappear, and neither did the Samaritans blend entirely with them. They all stayed there with all the idiomatic and cultural traits of their various origins, and their descendants still occupied the land during the days of Christ.

Now then, the captives of the Kingdom of Judah were repatriated by Cyrus, the King of Persia in the year 539 B.C. (2 Chronicles 36:23). Being that the Persians conquered the Babylonians, that in their day had conquered the Assyrians, the land that pertained to the other ten tribes was now under the dominion of the King of Persia.

Likewise, we understand that the Jews that King Cyrus had repatriated had also asked for his permission to occupy the territory that was the inheritance of the ten tribes of the north. In this manner, they would not yield the entire territory to the Gentiles. These people were now occupying the inheritance of the ten northern tribes that they had lost because of their consistent infidelity to the Lord. All this happened according to God's Word when He said:

> *Even when you have children and grandchildren and have grown old in that land, don't become corrupt and make carved idols or statues that represent anything. I call heaven and earth as witnesses against you today: If you do this thing that the Lord your God considers evil, making him furious, you will quickly disappear from the land*

*you're going to possess on the other side of the Jordan River. You won't live very long there. You'll be completely wiped out. The Lord will scatter you among the people of the world, and only a few of you will be left among the nations where the Lord will force you to live.* (Deuteronomy 4:25-27 GW)

Even though the Jews were zealous in their determination not to mix with the Gentiles, some form of daily contact with the world that surrounded them was inevitable and impossible to avoid, and for business, it was utterly impractical. A modicum of mundane involvement even in the political and social issues that surrounded and affected them was indispensable.

Among these Gentiles were Greeks, Syrophoenicians, Romans, descendants of the Assyrians, and other nations that we have mentioned. Of course, with all the ethnic groups and different nationalities of the region, theirs was naturally a multilingual world. They spoke Aramean and Hebrew, and Greek and Latin were very familiar to them as well as many other languages.

Two of the Apostles had Greek names: Andrew and Phillip. Three times John,[75] in his Gospel, calls Thomas,[76] Didymus,[77] a literal translation of the Hebrew (Aramaic) to Greek for "twin." Even though it could have been that many were not exactly fluent in some of these languages, it most certainly was not

---

[75] John 11:16, 20:24, 21:2
[76] Hebrew: *Thaom* – תאום
[77] Δίδυμος - *Didumos*

atypical for them to hear, understand or to communicate in a rudimentary manner in these tongues.

This influence of other cultures and languages was manifested in the given names and nicknames of the people, as has been illustrated with the examples of Andrew, Phillip, and Didymus. We can also see another example when Simon, Andrews brother, is referred to as Peter or Cephas, thus changing his moniker from one language to another with natural ease. Simon is his Hebrew name (-שׁמעון) translated into Greek (Σίμων). In Hebrew, it is *"Shimon"*, or *"Shimeon"*.

"Cephas" is pronounced *"Kēphas"* (Κηφᾶς). It is a Chaldean word, but it is very similar to the Hebrew word *"kef"* (כף), which means, *"rock, or cleft in a rock."* In another chapter, we will address John Mark's name, for it carries the same characteristics that are mentioned in this section.

### Now, Back to the "Marys"

I have taken the time to explain all this to illustrate the fact that the use of different names or the use of the same name in different languages, such as Saul and Paul, or Silas and Silvanus[78] was a common practice. Therefore, to find a family that would name their children in different languages, even though the names carried the same meaning, was not at all atypical.

Now then, in the book of Ruth, Noemi,[79] in her grief, told the people not to call her Neomi, but to call her now, by the moniker

---

[78] Greek: "Σιλουανός" (*Silouanos*), from the Latin, to be compared with the name "Σίλας" (Silas).

[79] Strong's, H5281 (נעמי) Agradable, un deleite.

of Mara: *"To whom she said, Do not ye call me Naomi, or Delightful, or Pleasant, but call ye me Mara, or Bitter; for Almighty God hath filled me with great bitterness..."* (Ruth 1:20 WYC).

In our case, we are talking about sisters from the same family from this region that had the same names derived from the word, "Mara"[80] (מרים).[81] Though we have already explained that one of the sisters full name was Mary Salome, and for all we know, the other simply known as Mary, in the distinct languages that were used in the region, these names were completely different. She could have been called Maria, from the Greek and the Latin. She could also have been called Miriam or *Mirjam*[82] from the Hebrew or Aramean. Alternatively, you could have called her Mara, and with the Greek translation, in this sense, it would be the same name, because it was merely the interpretation and the implication or significance of her name.

To illustrate the implications and interpretations of names, here in Spain we have the commonly used name of Maria. We also have Dolores (pains), and even Angustias (Anguish). (Wow!) In any case presented here, from the Hebrew-Aramaic root of Maria, we have the concept of these names; the name Mara. These other names are derived from the concept of Maria (which is bitterness). In Spain, these other names are given to identify the daughters of Catholic families to the Mary, the mother of Jesus, and all her suffering:

---

[80] Ibid. H4751 (מרה) mârâh, amargo, dolor, luto. Éxodo 15:23.
[81] Ibid. H4755 (מרא) Mara, amargura, Rut 1:20.
[82] Ibid. H4813 (מרים) *miryâm* – tomado de H4805, la palabra *"merîy"* (מרי) que en la Reina-Valera 1960 es traducida como "María".

> *Simeon blessed them. He said to Mary, the mother of Jesus, `He will be a sign that people do not believe in. He will make many people in Israel fall and rise. (Yes, a long knife will cut your heart too.) What people think will be made known'.* (Luke 2:34-35 WE).

What we have with these names is that the author has utilized the form of the name that was more familiar to the people that spoke the language in which he was writing. They gave them a Greek name with the Roman-Latin influences. We do the same thing with the names of almost all the Bible characters and places in English today. Jesus' name was "Yeshua," and not Jesus, but today we all know and love Him by a name by which He was not known in His day and country. For this reason, Miryam or Mirjam always comes out as Mary for us.

We can see the same influence of the Vulgate (Latin Bible) in the Greek in the Septuagint influenced by the Roman-Latin in the Old Testament Scriptures in the Douay-Rheims Bible: *"So Mary[83] the prophetess, the sister of Aaron, took a timbrel in her hand: and all the women went forth after her with timbrels and with dances."* (Exodus 15:20 DRB).

This is the version of the name taken directly from the Latin of the Vulgate. In this translation, you can see where they got the name, Mary. The Vulgate, this verse reads like this: *"sumpsit ergo Maria prophetis soror Aaron tympanum in manu*

---

[83] Ibid. H4813 hebreo (מרים) *miryâm.* Griego "μαριαμ" (*Mariam*). Latín "Maria"

*egressaeque sunt omnes mulieres post eam cum tympanis et choris"* (Exodus 15:20 Vulgate Latina)

Nevertheless, without the influence of the Septuagint or the Vulgate Latina but translated directly from the Hebrew we have: "*Then Miriam the prophetess, (Miryâm)*[84] *the sister of Aaron, took a tambourine in her hand, and all the women went out after her with tambourines and dancing.*" (ESV)

Better still is this translation directly from the Hebrew: "*And Miryam the prophetess, the sister of Aharon, took the timbrel in her hand. And all the women went out after her with timbrels and with dances...*" (Exodus 15:20 TS2009).

So then, to answer this question that John 19:25 provokes: "How can we have two sisters with the name Mary?" We first consider the region in which they lived, and the sociocultural history of the zone, which we can see was multiethnic and polyglot. We also observed that people of the same family had names that came from different languages, and that it was more important to understand the significance of a name rather than its phonetic appeal. This situation makes it possible that it could be the same significance, but in two different dialects of the region, they would be two different words, but principally we would have the same name.

### Back to the road to Emmaus

After reviewing the essential background information, we return to the reason we mentioned a Cleopas and Miryam (*or*

---

[84] Paréntesis del autor

*Mary*). However, at this point, it is necessary to ask another question: *"Why did Christ take the time to manifest himself to people that, it seems as if the Scriptures have never mentioned before, nor do we seem to hear about them afterward?"* It is certain that they were His followers and disciples, and we know that Christ appeared to more than five hundred of His disciples after His resurrection.[85] Nevertheless, *"Why pay this particular attention to mention these two?"*

We know that he appeared personally to His half-brother James. The result of this encounter was that James grew to become one of the most influential leaders of the Early Church and the author of the first book written for the New Testament.

The answer to the case of Cleopas and Miryam is found in the simple fact that they were the uncle and aunt of the Lord Jesus Christ. Their names were Cleopas Zebedee, and Miriam Salomé and they were a part of His earthly family. As has been mentioned, the son of this couple, Simeon, the son of Clopas, became the leader of the church of Jerusalem after the martyrdom of James, the half-brother of Christ.[86]

---

[85] 1ª Corintios 15:6 *"Then he appeared to more than five hundred brothers at one time, most of whom are still alive, though some have fallen asleep."*

[86] Eusebius of Caesarea, Church History, Book III, ch. 11.

# Chapter 5

# JOHN MARK

## The Relationship Between John Mark and Joseph of Cyprus

Before we can speak of the relationship between Mark and Joseph of Cyprus, we should know who Joseph was. The first time we find him in the Scriptures, he is presented simply as Joseph, a Levite born in Cyprus. Immediately, his kind and compassionate heart are manifested. We can also see his love for God and his work when he sold an inheritance that was in his possession and gave the money to the Apostles for the use of the work of the Lord in Jerusalem (Acts 4:36-37).

Seeing this, the Apostles honored him with the Aramean moniker, Bar Nebuah, or as we call him, Barnabas. From this point forward, we only know him by this nickname. Now, Bar Nebuah means "the son of the prophet" or, "The son of the prophecy." However, the church applied the literal meaning to convey the results of his actions giving it the implication of "The Son of Consolation." This nickname was more a title than a name because we can see that it was a clear indication of his characteristics as a consoler and a preacher.

It is also evident that the leaders of the church in Jerusalem had heard him preach Christ and expound on the virtues of the Scriptures. After all, he was a Levite, and the Law of Moses had declared that his family should be set apart for the Lord's service in the Temple. Therefore, it is understood that he would have had a sound knowledge of the Word of God.

The church in Antioch[87] also recognized the ministerial gift he possessed. *"Now there were in the church at Antioch certain prophets and teachers: Barnabas, and Simeon who was called Niger, and Lucius of Cyrene, and Manaen who had been brought up with Herod, the tetrarch, and Saul..."* (Acts 13:1 KJ21). It is interesting to notice that Barnabas is the first one mentioned in this list. I believe that it is an indication that, at that time, he was the one that had the most fluid and dynamic gift of leadership in the church.

As per being a consoler, we can see this when Saul, who had been preaching in Damascus after his conversion to Christ, had to leave because of the threats against his life. He returned to Jerusalem to join the Believers there, but none would receive him until Barnabas took him and presented him to the church.

> *When Saul arrived in Jerusalem, he tried to join the disciples, but they all were afraid of him because they wouldn't believe he was a disciple. Barnabas, however, introduced Saul to the apostles, telling them how on the road Saul had seen the Lord, who had spoken to him, and how*

---

[87] Antioch today is the city of Antakya, Turkey.

*courageously he had spoken in the name of Jesus in Damascus.* (Acts 9:26-27 ISV)

When Barnabas was commissioned by the church in Jerusalem to oversee the work in Antioch, the Bible, once again, indicates that Barnabas *"... was a good man, full of the Holy Spirit and faith. And so, a large number of people was brought to the Lord..."* (Acts 11:24 IVS). Barnabas recognized that the gift that Saul had to teach the Scriptures could be of great use and edification for the church in Antioch. Therefore, Acts 11:25 says that He went to Tarsus to find Saul and to take him to help minister in the church in Antioch. It was there, under the ministerial direction of Barnabas in Antioch, that the disciples were first called Christians (Acts 11:26).

The last part of Acts chapter 11, the prophet Agabus received a prophetic word that a famine was coming over the earth. The brethren in Antioch decided to send an offering to the church in Judea. Now, this is mere speculation on my part, but seeing Barnabas' history of generosity and merciful kindheartedness showed to the church while in Jerusalem, he very well could have been the person that suggested to send an offering from the church in Antioch. The church agreed and decided to send Barnabas and Saul to take the offering.

When their mission in Jerusalem was completed, and it was time to return to Antioch, they took with them John, *"whose other name was Mark"* (ESV).

## Barnabas; The Leader-Maker

A short time after their return, a prophetic word was given that said that Barnabas and Saul should be set apart for ministry as missionaries, as so it was. However, Saul was commissioned under the ministry and authority of Barnabas:

> *As they were worshipping the Lord and fasting, the Holy Spirit said, "Appoint Barnabas and Saul to the work I have called them to undertake." After they fasted and prayed, they laid their hands on these two and sent them off.* (Acts 13:2-3 CEB)

Barnabas and Saul were especially apt for the work to which God had called them, because both were born, and were raised in foreign countries, and were accustomed to living and associating among the Gentiles.

As has been said, Barnabas was from Cyprus. Cyprus is an island that, in the days of Mark, had more than a thousand years of history. The small island had more than a hundred archeological settlements that dated back to the years 3000 B.C. and 2500 B.C. At that time, the island, because of consecutive invasions, it had become the home of the Hittites, Phoenicians, Greeks, Assyrians, Persians, Egyptians, Romans, and Arabs. The island was (and continues to be) an encounter points for Asia, Africa, and Europe, and all these places have left the marks of their presence on the island itself, and in its inhabitants.

Saul was from Tarsus, the capital city of the Roman province of Cilicia, that was found on the southern coast of Asia Minor.

Today, the whole area is in the country of Turkey. This region had the same characteristics as the island of Cyprus, in that being a place with a lengthy historical background, it was multiethnic and pluricultural. Being born in the region of Cilicia also made Saul a natural born Roman citizen, and Paul is his Roman name.

This calling was a confirmation of what the Lord had told him the day that he surrendered his life to Christ's Lordship:

> *Stand up! I have appeared to you for a reason. I'm appointing you to be a servant and witness of what you have seen and of what I will show you. I will rescue you from the Jewish people and from the non-Jewish people to whom I am sending you. You will open their eyes and turn them from darkness to light and from Satan's control to God's. Then they will receive forgiveness for their sins and a share among God's people who are made holy by believing in me.'* (Acts 26:16-18 GW)[88]

John Mark accompanied them during the first part of this journey, but soon, he abandoned his post and returned to Jerusalem (Acts 13:13).

Later, in Acts 15, they decided to make a second missionary journey to consolidate the works that they had established. Barnabas wanted to give a second opportunity to John Mark, but Paul thought that Mark was not yet ready to go with them.

---

[88] See also Acts 9:15-16.

*John Mark: The author of the first Gospel*

Consequently, Barnabas took John Mark to Cyprus, and Paul took Silas with him.

We can only speculate as to when the church in Cyprus was established, but, historically, Barnabas is considered to be the founder of that church. The birth of the Cyprian church, very well, could have been the fruit of this missionary endeavor with John Mark.

Being that in the prior ministerial endeavors, the commissioned missionary in charge was Barnabas, because he had his seal of recognition, blessing, and support of the church. Paul was under his charge and authority. Now, it was Paul's time to receive his commission and the recognition of his ministry. Hence, we see the church give him his formal charge and commission, and, as has been said, he chose to take Silas with him and under his responsibility. Thanks to the blessing of Barnabas' ministry and discipleship, Paul has his ministry and has an established recognition as a leader in the church.

I agree with John Piper in his thoughts on Barnabas' virtue.[89] It is also my thought that Joseph of Cyprus is famous in the Scriptures for being a leader-maker. As we have seen, there are two notable leaders and heroes in the church that were formed by his discipleship and direct influence: Saul of Tarsus, and John, *"whose other name was Mark."* I am sure that if we knew more details of history, we would find a plethora more of leaders that came about as a result of the fruit of his ministry.

---

[89] John Piper, *Barnabas: A Maker of Leaders*, Desiring God, Topic: New Testament Biblical Figures https://www.desiringgod.org/messages/barnabas-the-maker-of-a-great-leader?lang=es. July 12, 1987. (Accessed 02/07/2019)

These testimonies are just another proof that he was deserving of the nickname Barnabas, "The Son of Consolation."

We know that Colossians 4:10 states that John Mark was a relative of Barnabas.[90] However, I want to underscore something here; I do not want to be dogmatic on this point. I merely want to present the argument that favors the relationship of maternal uncle and nephew between Barnabas and John Mark. I understand the academics of that incline an interpretation of the relationship of cousins between the two, and I recognize the possibility that this could very well have been what it was. Nevertheless, as are many such things in our ambiance, there are also strong points that favor the relationship that I embrace. Therefore, in benefit and the edification of all, here I will present them.

"The Cambridge Bible for Schools and Colleges," was the first ever complete commentary set to be published by Cambridge University Press. The more than thirty theologians and biblical scholars that contributed to this collection held this opinion about Colossians 4:10:

> ... Mary the mother of John, whose surname was Mark] This Mary was sister to Barnabas, as we learn Col. 4:10, where Mark is called sister's son to Barnabas. This relationship accounts for the way in which the uncle clung to his nephew, even when

---

[90] "*Aristarchus my fellow prisoner saluteth you, and also Mark, Barnabas' sister's son (concerning whom ye received instructions that if he come unto you, receive him),*" (Colossians 4:10 KJ21)

> *St Paul declined to have Mark as a companion on their second proposed missionary journey.*[91]

The Greek term of Colossians helps us to understand the relationship between Barnabas and John Mark a little bit more clearly; because when Paul says, "... *the cousin of Barnabas...*" (MEV), As is found in most English translations. We also have, "... *Mark, nephew to Barnabas...*" (JUB) Which we find in fewer translations in English. Added to these translations, find the even the more generic form of the Greek word that we find in a few translations such as, "... *Mark, a relative of Barnabas...*" (TLB), which we also find in several English translations. This dilemma is interesting because the Greek word that Paul used here is "*anepsios*" (ἀνέψιος). This work can mean "*the son of a sister*", but it can also be utilized for the English word "*cousin*".

The academic world is historically divided over the application of the word "ἀνέψιος". As has been said, there are solid viewpoints for both interpretations, and both expressions explain the attitudes and actions taken by Joseph in the book of Acts; which attitudes and actions we will discuss in detail further ahead.

One of the most persuasive arguments to accept the interpretation of this word as "cousin" is the use of the word "ἀνέψιος" in the Septuagint in Numbers 36:11, "*For Mahlah, Tirzah, and*

---

[91] J.R. Lumby, *The Cambridge Bible for Schools and Colleges* - the first commentary set published by Cambridge University Press. Published 1882-1921 Public Domain.

*Hoglah, and Milcah, and Noah, the daughters of Zelophehad, were married unto their fathers brothers' sons..."*⁹²

Then again, there are cases in which scholars, such as John Gill in his work, "*The New John Gill Exposition of the Entire Bible*,"⁹³ supports the idea that it is better interpreted as "nephew," by calling Mary, Barnabas' sister. Robert Jamieson, Andrew Robert Fausset, and David Brown in their historical commentary, "*Jamieson, Fausset and Brown Commentary*," also incline towards the translation of nephew.⁹⁴

The Vulgate translates Colossians 4:10 with the Latin word "*consobrinues*,"⁹⁵ which means, "nephew." Of the three possible interpretations of "*consobrinus*," or, "*consobrini*," the first, meaning, the most dominant word in its forthright use, is that of "nephew."

Other contemporary academics such as Dr. Robert Plummer,⁹⁶ of whom I consider to be a brilliant koine Greek scholar, and professor of New Testament Interpretation at the Southern

---

⁹² "καὶ ἐγένοντο Θερσα καὶ Εγλα καὶ Μελχα καὶ Νουα καὶ Μααλα θυγατέρες Σαλπααδ τοῖς ἀνεψιοῖς αὐτῶν·" (Numbers 36:11 Greek OT)

⁹³ John Gill, "*Commentary on Colossians 4:10; The New John Gill Exposition of the Entire Bible*". 1748-1763, 1809; *Public Domain*. Baker Book House, 2768 East Paris Ave. SE, Grand Rapids, MI 49546, 1980.

⁹⁴ Robert Jamieson, Andrew Robert Fausset, y David Brown, *Jamieson, Fausset and Brown Commentary*, *Public Domain*, originally published in 1871.

⁹⁵ Latdict, Latin Dictionary & Grammar Resources. Latin definition for: *consobrinus, consobrini*, http://latin-dictionary.net/definition/13407/consobrinus-consobrini. (Accessed 12/12/2018).

⁹⁶ Robert L. Plummer, *The Gospel According to St. Mark; Background*, Birmingham Theological Seminary, http://es.btsfreeccm.org/local/lmp/lessons.php?lesson=GOS3text. 2200 Briarwood Way, Birmingham, AL 35243-2923. © 2012. (Accessed 17-12-2018).

Baptist Theological Seminary, and Dr. Mark Strauss,[97] a professor of New Testament at Bethel University affirm that John Mark is the nephew of Barnabas.

In the same way, Dr. Albert Barns, in his commentary, *Notes on the New Testament: Matthew and Mark*,[98] is also of the school of thought that Mark was the son of Barnabas' sister.

Most of the historical translators of the book of Acts of the Apostles, in Castilian, support the interpretation that the correct application is that of a nephew.

It is interesting to read the opinion of Dr. Marvin Vincent, on Colossians 4:10,[99] saying that he preferred the application of the word "cousin," because the use of the term "nephew" is, historically more recent. He is correct that in many of the English translations (the native language of Dr. Vincent) you will find that, at least eight of ten of the modern translations back his view.

Nevertheless, to do the same in other languages, such as Spanish, we will find that the exact opposite is true. Because, the application of cousin is found only in the more recent translations, and nephew in the older historical versions.

However, even concerning English, I respectfully find Dr. Vincent a tad bit inaccurate, historically speaking. Apart from

---

[97] Mark Strauss, *The Gospel According to St. Mark; Background*, Birmingham Theological Seminary, http://es.btsfreeccm.org/local/lmp/lessons.php?lesson=GOS3text. 2200 Briarwood Way, Birmingham, AL 35243-2923. © 2012. (Accessed 17-12-2018).

[98] Albert Barns, *Notes on the New Testament: Matthew and Mark*, Baker Book House, Grand Rapids, MI 1954.

[99] Marvin R. Vincent, "*Vincent's Word Studies in the New Testament; Commentary on Colossians 4:10*", New York: Charles Schribner's Sons. 1887. https://www.studylight.org/commentaries/vnt/colossians-4.html. (Accessed 12/12/2018).

the King James Authorized Version (1611), we must take into consideration that there are many classical-historical translations by reputable scholars that are of the "nephew" school of thought. Translations such as:

- The Daniel Mace New Testament (1729),
- John Wesley New Testament (1755),
- John Worsley New Testament (1770),
- Thomas Haweis New Testament (1795),
- The Noah Webster's Bible (1833),
- Sawyer New Testament (1858),
- The Young's Literal Translation (1862),
- Julia Evelina Smith Parker Translation (1876), to name a few.

Just as in these examples, we can see that the same is found in a plethora of translations and viewpoints. Therefore, let us merely say that there are these two excellent, and orthodox postures concerning this point of Barnabas' relation to John Mark. However, I want you to know that, for reasons that will become evident, I am of the school of thought that John Mark is Barnabas' nephew.

One interesting point to bring out is that etymologically, many philologists will say that the word "ἀνέψιος" is the root of the English word for "nephew," and not "cousin." The English language has been developed from the Greek, Latin, Germanic, and Anglo-Saxon roots.

Even though we could continue to speculate in this study of the word ἀνέψιος, we must concede that the word was not written in a historical and situational vacuum. Therefore, the correct way to proceed would be to do an exegesis on all that we could on Mark, Joseph of Cyprus, and all the other people and situations involved to properly understand its correct context.

My last comment on this subject is entirely from a personal, and not an academic perspective. It is that I perceive that we are seeing that the relational attitude that Barnabas has towards Mark is that of an older family member to a younger one. I find Barnabas looking out for Mark as an uncle would look out for a nephew that was given into his charge. It is more that of a loving and doting uncle over his neophyte nephew. The dynamics seem different from those that might present themselves between cousins, which, to me, would be a relationship that would be far more reciprocal.

Now then, I admit that this point does not deny the possibility of such a relationship between cousins. Nevertheless, we can find another similar Biblical situation that brings an argument in favor of cousins to this point. I am talking about the case between the cousins Mordecai and Hadassah. However, it is reasonable and correct that a male member of the family would be protective, looking out for and being far more defensive for a female member of the family; especially a much younger and orphaned female cousin. Though not conclusive, in this, we can find a difference in the situations.

Nevertheless, after having contemplated this point, we shall continue forward to study other relationships in the life of Mark. With them, we will try to understand the situational context of what we read about these notably prominent New Testament personalities.

## Chapter 6

# JOHN MARK'S MOTHER

We have covered several points in which we have had to mention John Mark's mother, and in doing so, we have learned much about her. However, even though it be in a summary fashion, it is necessary to dedicate a section to focus on her.

We know through Acts 12:12, that her name was Mary. Being that she had, at least, one child, John Mark and that she was a respected member of the church, and in a good relationship with her family, we might assume one of two things:

- 1.) That she was married.
- 2.) That she was widowed.

As per her other possible condition, that she might be a widow, we must recognize that the Bible holds great respect for widows. Exodus 22:22 says: *"You are not to abuse any widow or orphan..."* (CJB). In the Early Church, they had a ministry established to assure that the widows were cared for and respected. This is the reason that the ministry of the deacon was established in Acts 6.[100] We have a Pauline command to honor the

---

[100] Acts 9:39; 1ª Timoteo 5:5-16;

widows in I Timothy 5:3: "*Honor widows who are truly widows...*" (JBS). James 1:27, also gives a similar injunction: "*Pure religion and undefiled before our God and Father is this, to visit the fatherless and widows in their affliction, and to keep oneself unspotted from the world...*" (ASV).

I want to take Zeruah, the mother of Jeroboam, for an example to illustrate this respectful attention that the Bible gives to widows. Though after mentioning her in 1 Kings 11:26, the Bible never mentions her again; her son became the first king of the Northern Kingdom. "*Jeroboam, Solomon's servant, the son of Nebat, an Ephrathite of Zeredah whose mother's name was Zeruah, a widow, also rebelled against the king...*" (NVI).

Even though Zeruah's son became an evil King that rebelled against Jehovah more than against the House of David, the Bible speaks no evil of her. We can see this pattern of respect throughout the Bible. The Hebrew word "widow" is "*'almânâh,*" and it is mentioned fifty-five times in the Old Testament. The Greek word "widow" is, "*chēra*" (χήρα), and it is found twenty-six times in the New Testament. So, from what we can see in all these cases when a woman was a widow, it is always mentioned or alluded to so as not to miss any significant detail concerning her. An example of an allusion to widowhood and not a direct comment is the commission that Christ gave to the Apostle John from the cross in John 19:26-27:

> *When Jesus, therefore, saw his mother, and the disciple standing by, whom he loved, he saith unto his mother, Woman, behold thy son! Then saith he to the disciple, Behold thy mother! And from that*

*hour that disciple took her unto his own home.* (BRG)

Widowhood would have been an important detail to include concerning the mother of John Mark if she, in truth, was a widow.

Nevertheless, no such detail ever comes out about this when it mentions her name for the first time; and her son turned out to be a great servant of God. Imagine the excellent example of I Timothy 5:3-16 for the church that she would have been. However, being that this detail is omitted in the description of Mary, the mother of John Mark, I believe that we can Biblically assume that she was not a widow, but that she was married.

Being that I conclude that Mary, John Mark's mother was not a widow, but was married, I also want to present my position that I believe that Simon Peter was her husband and consequently, was also the biological father of John Mark. From this point forward, I will build the foundation of my argument.

Concerning the house mentioned in Acts 12:12, as we have said, at this point, for almost four hundred years the conviction was installed into the Jewish families to acquire housing or property in or Jerusalem. These would become family inheritances such as Joseph of Cyprus sold and gave to the church. As is typical, some families prospered and had accumulated more than others.

Also, as we have indicated, it is believed that Mary, John Mark's mother was Joseph of Cyprus' sister. (Once again, I will say that if Mary is Barnabas' sister, John Mark is his nephew.) Mary, very possibly, was also from Cyprus. We know that Joseph sold an inheritance and gave the earnings to the Lord, but, that does not mean that it was the only property that his family owned. Some scholars believe that the house of Mary in Acts 12, was another piece of property that the family owned.

Today, many Jewish scholars in Israel believe that Simon Peter's house in Capernaum was actually the home of Peter's mother-in-law. I am not of that thought; I think that it was his home and that his mother-in-law lived with him in her widowed old age. Nevertheless, it is still rather interesting none the less, and it also goes to my point that the wealth of Barnabas' family is a well-considered idea, or fact, among theologians and Biblical historians. I will say that the house in Acts 12 could also have been the property of Simon Peter's family; both ideas are perfectly reasonable concepts. At any rate, I believe that the fact that Peter considered this the first place to go is evidence that he was very familiar with the house.

Now the question is raised is not concerning prosperity, but "how did Simon, the son of Jonah of Capernaum get married to Mary from Cyprus? I want to answer this question with an illustration: I began my ministry here in Spain near the end of the 1980s, and the beginning of the 90s. (Wow! Saying it like that makes it sound like a long time ago.) At that time, the evangelicals numbered less than one-tenth of one percent of the population of forty-five million people. I pastored a church of about thirty people, and they were just about all young people, and most of them were single young ladies.

There were so few churches that, to avoid the plague of unequally yoked marriages, one of the only ways that the youth could find marriage partners was at the national youth congresses, and other reunions of churches from different parts of the provinces, or of the nation. At times we would see things like married couples where the husband was from País Vasco, and the wife from Cádiz or the husband was from Barcelona and the wife from the Canary Islands. How? It was because of the youth congresses.

Now, take into consideration the situation of the Jews from the Galilean region. There are many towns and villages, and a few cities, but, for the average family, daily life was centered principally in the village, town, or city in which you lived. That goes without mentioning:

- The dangers of bands of thieves by the roadsides,
- The available means of transportation,
- The roads and paths of that day,
- The average distance between populations,
- The time it took to walk from one place to another with the entire family,
- The expenses involved, and,
- The inconvenience because of the plethora of inconveniences involved because of other innumerable logistical details entailed.

It was not a typical family outing to go from one town to another merely to pass the time or take a day off as we might do today. It had to be something of a large scale of importance. Merchants were those that did the most traveling, but their livelihood depended on it. Nevertheless, the farmers, sheep-herders, carpenters, potters, weavers, and other stock trades, by necessity, had to have more sedentary lifestyles.

This presented a problematical situation when it came to the time of meeting other families that were not already blood family members; of course, to avoid enter-marrying multiple generations within the same bloodlines. Therefore, when it came to finding a spouse for your son or daughter, distant travel was often the all-around most favorable option.

A spiritually and physically healthy way to do this was the annual Holy Feast Days celebrated in Jerusalem. All the faithfully religious families celebrated one or another of the holy days as frequently as they could. Which, at best might have been, in the most favorable of situations, once a year. Their families had made every effort to do so since the return from the Babylonian captivity and the establishment of the synagogues with the systematic teaching of the Law of Moses and the Prophets.

Good Jewish families from everywhere the diaspora had spread the Judean descendants, returned to Jerusalem to worship and to celebrate the Passover (Pesach), the Feast of Tabernacles (Sukkot), or any one of the other Holy Feast Days. Many of these families faced similar situations in the villages, towns, and cities where they lived.

In some places of the diaspora outside of the Judean and Galilean regions, the problem was even worse, for raw pagans that worshipped demonic gods surrounded the Jewish communities. So, it was reasonable that these families would come

## John Mark's Mother

with the hopes to establish a good relationship with another faithful Jewish family with whom they could establish marriage covenants for their marriage aged children. Therefore, it is evident that during one of these Holy Feast Days, that the family of Joseph and Mary of Cyprus, made a pact with the family of Jonah from Capernaum of the Galilean region.

The final point to this chapter; I have worked in countries and with cultures where arranged marriages are common. One of the conditions that they seek is an equal level of financial accommodation from the family with which the covenant is made. In other words, if Mary of Cyprus were from a well-to-do family, her father would not have covenanted with a struggling, no hope, no future, no money, no trade, or job type of family.[101] Simon's family had to be of some means to have joined in a marriage covenant with the family of Joseph and Mary of Cyprus.

An important detail in these cultures is the dowry or bride price. This is not, as some would suppose, the act of buying a bride, it is a manifestation of how this man can provide for and support his wife and family. It is a display or an indication of his means. A family cannot demand more than they already provide, or their present level of living. Consequently, the dowry must be equal to this level or better by the offer of the husband's family.

---

[101] Just a question: *How many of you would like for your daughter to marry to some "dude" with no job, no money, no education, no plans, no future, and so on...?* No, it is normal to make sure that your daughters are well cared for once they are married.

Chapter 7

# THE RELATIONSHIP BETWEEN JOHN MARK AND PAUL

*Paul did not change his name when he embraced the faith in Jesus Christ as Israel's Messiah y Savior pf the Gentiles, but, as a Roman of his era, he already had what was called a praenomen[102] related with a family characteristic (Saul, his Jewish name, that etymologically means 'invoked', or "called'), and a cognomen, the only name used in the epistles (Paulus, his Roman name, that etymologically means 'small' or 'little').[103]*

## Background

The book of Acts tells us that after Stephen's death, the church in Jerusalem experienced a diaspora of its congregation. Even though it was not intentional on the church's behalf, it was the way that the Holy Spirit employed to begin

---

[102] Praenomen: The first name, or personal name given in ancient Rome. For example: *Marcus* Tullius Cicero.

[103] Rinaldo Fabris, *Pablo: el apóstol de los gentiles (Paul: The Apostle to the Gentiles)*. 1999. Ediciones San Pablo, Protasio Gómez, 15, 28027 Madrid.

the fulfillment of the Great Commission that Christ gave the church in Acts 1:8: "... *But you will receive power when the Holy Spirit has come on you, and you will be my witnesses in Jerusalem, in all Judea and Samaria, and to the end of the earth,*" (CSB).

After the Day of Pentecost, the church experienced a great revival and a spiritual awakening for the city. Thousands were added to the people of God. Nevertheless, the blessing did not come so that the church could celebrate a continuous 'feel good' party with one another. Instead, it came to give the power to take the Gospel to the whole world. Mark 16:15-18 says:

> *He said to them, "Go into the whole world and proclaim the good news to every creature. Whoever believes and is baptized will be saved, but whoever doesn't believe will be condemned. These signs will be associated with those who believe they will throw out demons in my name. They will speak in new languages. They will pick up snakes with their hands. If they drink anything poisonous, it will not hurt them. They will place their hands on the sick, and they will get well."* (CEB)

Acts 11:19 informs us that:

> *They then who had been scattered abroad through the tribulation that took place on the occasion of Stephen, passed through [the country] to Phoenicia and Cyprus and Antioch, speaking the word to no one but to Jews alone.* (CJB)

Remember, that Stephen was one of the Greek deacons called to serve and minister to the Greek widows (Acts 6:1-5).

> *A lot of people were now becoming followers of the Lord. But some of the ones who spoke Greek started complaining about the ones who spoke Aramaic. They complained that the Greek-speaking widows were not given their share when the food supplies were handed out each day. The twelve apostles called the whole group of followers together and said, "We should not give up preaching God's message in order to serve at tables. My friends, choose seven men who are respected and wise and filled with God's Spirit. We will put them in charge of these things. We can spend our time praying and serving God by preaching." This suggestion pleased everyone, and they began by choosing Stephen. He had great faith and was filled with the Holy Spirit. Then they chose Philip, Prochorus, Nicanor, Timon, Parmenas, and also Nicolaus, who worshiped with the Jewish people in Antioch.* (CEV)

The persecution that followed the death of Stephen fell, principally, over the Greek Jews. Acts 8:1 says:

> *And Saul was consenting to his being killed. And on that day there arose a great persecution against the assembly which was in Jerusalem, and*

*all were scattered into the countries of Judaea and Samaria except the apostles.* (DARBY)

We should not think that Luke was saying to us that all the Believers had left Jerusalem and that the only ones that were left were the twelve Apostles listening to the crickets chirping. Instead, in a general sense, the Greeks had to leave Jerusalem to save their lives.

Even still, there were some zealous and daring Believers from Cyprus and Cyrene (from Libya, Africa) that spoke to all those that would hear them.

> *But there were some of them— Cyprian and Cyrenian men— who, having come to Antioch, were speaking also to the Hellenists, announcing-as-good-news the Lord Jesus. 21 And the hand of the Lord was with them. And a large number, having believed, turned to the Lord.* (Acts 11:20-21 DLNT)

When we read this, we must consider that the majority of those that had to leave Jerusalem were Greek Jews, just as was Stephen, the martyr, and just like Phillip the deacon, that was now doing the work of an evangelist in Acts 8:4-5: *"They therefore that were dispersed, went about preaching the word of God. And Philip going down to the city of Samaria preached Christ unto them..."* (DRA).

Therefore, we can confidently presume that it was these Greek Jews that had joyfully filled the church but were eventually spread abroad. I believe that they were speaking primarily to Greek God-Fearers, meaning uncircumcised gentiles that went to the synagogues to hear the teachings of the Law and the Prophets but had not yet become proselytes. These testimonies of the spread of the Gospel in the area of Antioch began to come back to the church in Jerusalem, and they sent Barnabas to investigate and confirm the situation.

Barnabas, seeing the mighty work of God in Antioch, decided that Saul could be a useful instrument in the edification of the church in that city. So, he departed to Tarsus, found Saul, and brought him back to serve in the church in Antioch.

## Barnabas, Paul, and John Mark

After a few years, they were sent to Jerusalem to fulfill a commission of the church in Antioch. They had the mission to present an important offering to help the Believers in need in Judea. When they returned home, Barnabas and Saul took John Mark with them, (Acts 12:25).

From what we know of our person of interest, this was the first time that John had left his native environment. He had lived his entire life in the regions of Galilee and Judea. Moreover, there is something significant that we must consider, and this is that Mary, his mother, and Barnabas, his uncle were Jews from Cyprus and they were very accustomed to being around Gentiles. As we have mentioned, Saul was also born and raised in the diaspora and grew up surrounded by Gentiles.

However, Mark was a Jew born in the land that the Romans had decided to name Palestine and his whole life he had lived surrounded by Jews. The Gentiles were there, but seen more from a distance and, as was their custom, they were seen as unclean. Surely, he had never been in the home of a Gentile, and neither had he ever hosted, or seen a Gentile hosted in his home. Remember the words of Peter, Mark's father, after God had called him specifically to go into the house of Cornelius?

> ... Ye know how that it is an abominable thing for a man that is a Jew to keep company or come unto one of another nation; but God has showed me that I should not call any man common or unclean, (Acts 10:28 JUB).

This information about John Mark's background is indispensable to keep in mind to understand certain events in his life that provoked his decision to abandon the work and the ensuing period of separation from Paul.

The logical conclusion to which I come when considering Mark's abandonment of the work in the early stages of his life and ministry is that it was an extreme case of culture shock. It is something that almost every missionary has endured in one way or another during the first years of their ministry. Even though the regions of Galilee and Judea were pluricultural, the radical changes of location, ethnicities, the sudden and total immersion, summed with uncountable micro-situations assaulted his mind day and night, resulting in an unexpected psychological situation that was too difficult for the young disciple to assimilate.

Culture shock is a complicated subject for all missionaries. Sometimes it is more complicated to adjust to a culture that is similar than it is to a radically different one. I have Heard it described as being equivalent to rearranging the furniture of the living quarters of the blind.

Part of Mark's culture shock was the conflict of the puritanical Jewish concepts under which he was raised, and the obligation that he now had to associate, and live with uncircumcised Gentiles daily, and to love and treat them as his brethren as if they were his equals. Nevertheless, if he was to minister with his uncle and with Paul, this was his new reality.

Allow me to Paint a picture of what poor Mark might have gone through. Mark was in the first stages of his ministerial formation and spiritual maturity. The changes that he was experiencing were subsequently too challenging to tolerate at the point where he was in his life, and ministerial development.

After having been in Antioch for some time, and still in the process of adjusting to this sociocultural change, a prophetic word was given in Acts 13:2, that separated Barnabas and Saul for the work that the Lord had for them. John Mark had gone out from the Jerusalem church as a disciple of his uncle, Joseph Barnabas. Therefore, officially, he was a part of Barnabas and Saul's team on their first missionary journey (Acts 13:5).

This was the beginning of another completely new stage in the life of the young John Mark. He left with his uncle and his faithful companion and disciple, Saul, to evangelize the Gentiles. In the beginning, in his mind, everything was a romantic idea and a thrilling adventure.

From Antioch, they traveled a short distance to the city of Seleucia, and then, on to Cyprus. This too probably thrilled Mark, because he had family there. However, being his first time on the open sea, he probably got sea-sick. This was not the Sea of Galilee! Culture shock and homesickness added to these things, and misery began to seep into John Mark's heart. Everything was strange, and everybody was a stranger. He was getting to know Paul, and he probably thought him to be a bit too strict and inflexible.

Also, his uncle seemed different now that he was seeing him in these foreign environments. He mixed so easily with the Gentiles and those of other nations that did not know God. Mark was a long way from home and getting farther every day. How could they not feel unclean after having so much contact with Gentiles? The different smells of the market places made his head spin. The odors of cooked swine's flesh, crabs, and other shelled animals were being boiled, along with other unclean sea and land creatures that were being roasted on open fires. It was repugnant to see these Gentiles eat such horrid beasts with so much glee and pleasure savoring and sucking even the bones.

When they arrived in Cyprus, it was refreshing to see his cousins. It was a joy to see his cousins and other family members; several of them were young people of his age and orthodox Jews. However, now he was seeing them in their natural Cypriot environment, enjoying themselves with him, but completely unaffected by all that surrounded them as if this was something normal.

The breaking point came after they arrived at Paphos, and a Jew came out to receive them, but this Jew was a warlock! Worse still, the warlock was named Bar-Jesus (the son of Jesus). This apostate Jew was in the constant company of a Roman proconsul named Sergius Paulus, an educated and prudent man (Acts 13:4-12).

Sergius Paulus desired to hear the Word of God, and he called Barnabas and Saul to speak with them and hear what they had to say. In their efforts to amply spread the Gospel by way of the positive influence they could have in the life of this important man, Barnabas and Paul formed a close friendship with him. This, most surely, involved going to his house, and very possibly, eating with him. However, as Sergius Paulus tried to hear the Word of God, Elymas, that is to say, Bar-Jesus, reprobate in his heresy, opposed every advance of Barnabas and Paul to minister the Word of Life to this man. He would continually interfere and put stumbling blocks before him.

It came to Mark's mind that which had happened to his father, Peter when he went to the house of Cornelius, the Roman centurion. Nevertheless, at least Cornelius was a God-Fearer and was accustomed, open, and adjusted to all that pertained to Judea and the Jews.

Even still, Peter only went after he saw the same vision three times in a row to convince him and tell him what he had to do. The result of his visit and time of ministry with Cornelius was that everybody received the Baptism in the Holy Spirit, spoke in tongues and glorified God. Even after all that, the church in Jerusalem rebuked his father. It was with great difficulty that they calmed down to hear the beautiful testimony of the work of God in the lives of Cornelius, his family, and friends (Acts 11:1-3).

In this case, a heretical Jew comes out to meet them accompanied by a Roman that knows nothing of Judaism. This was the worst scenario that he could imagine and added to everything else; it was more than he could tolerate. Sadly, Mark abandoned the work with these valiant pioneers and returned home (Acts 13:13).

After a successful missionary trip, they returned to the mother church in Antioch and testified of how God had opened the doors to minister to the Gentiles with so much success, (Acts 14:26-27). However, a problem arose when some from Judea did not accept that Justification by faith was sufficient for the conversion of the Gentiles. They argued that it was still necessary to pass through the whole process of proselytism and circumcision to become true Jewish converts. Paul and Barnabas reasoned that the justification by the grace of God and faith in Christ was the complete process to receive all the provision of God for salvation (Acts 15:1-2).

Therefore, once again, the church in Antioch commissioned Paul and Barnabas, together with other elders from their congregation to go up to Jerusalem to discuss this matter with the Apostles. This was the first Council of the church, and it was James that presided. He judged that Peter, Paul, and Barnabas were correct in their assessment of the situation with the Gentile converts.

An official letter was written and given into the hands of Paul and Barnabas to read in all the churches that minister to the Gentiles for Christ. Furthermore, to give a Little bit more authority to the letter, and as a proof of the total support of the

Apostles, they sent Judas and Silas with them. These two were prophets in the church in Jerusalem (Acts 15:27-35). While they were in Jerusalem, they found John Mark, and he returned to Antioch with them.

After some time, Judas felt that it was his time to return to Jerusalem, but Silas decided that he should stay in Antioch and continue his ministry there. During this time, Paul began to feel in his heart that they should return and minister to confirm the churches that they had established in their first missionary journey. Barnabas agreed but wanted to try again with John Mark. As we know, Paul felt that Mark was not yet ready to accompany them and that Silas was a far more mature candidate for the work. Barnabas was resolute. He was sure that Mark was a Good disciple and was willing to be corrected and trained to be fit for this kind of ministry.

Consequently, even though they were not in agreement as to have Mark as a part of their team, they agreed that it would be better if Barnabas took Mark to disciple him and to train him to be apt for the work. The truth is that even Barnabas recognized that he had to take much more time to develop the young disciple, but he was sure that his time and investment was worth the effort; that one day, Mark would be a great instrument in the hands of God. On the other hand, Paul had the burden for the immediate care of the new churches that were the fruit of their first missionary journey. Therefore, it was much more expedient for him to take Silas.

The church agreed with the decision that they had taken and being that Barnabas was already approved and commissioned, he took Mark and sailed to Cyprus. In this way, now Paul received his commission from the church and was able to establish his own ministry (Acts 15:40).

Barnabas did well to take Mark to Cyprus because it was there that Mark began the excellent training under the leadership of his uncle. The labor was proven to be the actual work of God. One evidence of Barnabas' work of discipleship in Mark is that afterward, we see John Mark working, once again, with Paul. He was with him to the point of suffering the hardships of prison with him in Rome. In the book of Philemon, a letter written from a prison cell, Paul writes in verses 23-24: *"Epaphras, my fellow prisoner in Christ Jesus, sends his greetings to you, as do Mark, Aristarchus, Demas, and Luke, my coworkers."* (EHV).

In the same way, in Colossians 4:10, a verse that we have seen many times in this study, Paul gives a recommendation that displays his sincere love for Mark and his wholehearted approval of the efficaciousness of his ministry. He also recognized that it was the fruit of the ministry of Mark's beloved uncle, Barnabas, saying: *"Salute you doth Aristarchus, my fellow-captive, and Marcus, the nephew of Barnabas, (concerning whom ye did receive commands—if he may come unto you receive him,)"* (YLT).

So effective was this time of discipleship with Barnabas that Paul asks Timothy to bring Mark with him because he was "useful." II Timothy 4:11: *"Luke alone is with me. Get Mark and bring him with you, for he is very useful to me for ministry..."* (ESV).

Now that is a success story!

## Chapter 8

# THE RELATIONSHIP BETWEEN SIMON PETER AND JOHN MARK

*She who is at Babylon, who is likewise chosen, sends you greetings, and so does Mark, my son.* (1 Peter 5:13 ESVUK)

*And as he considered the thing, he came to the house of Mary, the mother of John, whose surname was Mark, where many were gathered together, and prayed.* (Acts 12:12 GNV)

Though we have already mentioned the biological paternity of Pete to John Mark, I want to dedicate this section to finish applying the details to what I believe to be a Biblical fact.

I affirm the fact that I believe that Simon Peter was also the spiritual father of John Mark. This should not be anything atypical nor contradictory, because it is hoped that a Christian father would always also be the spiritual father, priest of his home, the absolute best example of a Christian, the greatest hero and rock star in the eyes of his children. At least, this is how it should be, and I do believe that it was this way with the beloved Apostle.

In our case, I am the biological and the spiritual father of my (adult) children. This is also nothing extraordinary. We all know Christian families whose children have come to be great servants of the Lord that indicate that they were the fruit of their parent's discipleship and in-the-flesh-examples of sincere servants of the Lord. Why should we not expect to see this among the protagonists of the New Testament?

It is evident that the Apostle Peter was a married man just like most of the other Apostles. Here, it is necessary to repeat a Scripture that we have reviewed before: *"Don't I have the right to follow the example of the other apostles and the Lord's brothers and Peter, by taking a Christian wife with me on my trips?"* (1 Corinthians 9:5 GNT).

At this point, I want to underscore what we already know about the confirmed relationship between Peter and Mark. Papias the bishop of Hierapolis,[104] Irenaeus,[105] Justin Martyr,[106] Clement of Alexandria,[107] Eusebius of Caesarea,[108] Tertullian,[109] and Origen of Alexandria attributed Mark's Gospel to Peter.[110] All historically, and irrevocably affirmed the close relationship between Peter and John Mark.

---

[104] Papias de Hierápolis, *Libro de Historia Eclesiástica II.* Chapter XV, Libro III, del Chapter XXX, y Libro VI, Chapter XIV.

[105] Irenaeus, *Against the Heresies.* (Book III Chapter I)

[106] Justino Mártir, *"Diálogo con Trifón"*

[107] Clemente de Alejandría, *"Hypotyposeis"* (*Historia Eclesiástica*, Libro II Chapter XV)

[108] Eusebius de Cesarea, , Ἐκκλησιαστικὴ ἱστορία, (*Historia Eclesiástica*), Libro VI Chapter XIV.

[109] Tertullian, *"Against Marcion"*, Book IV Chapter V.; New Advent: http://www.newadvent.org/fathers/0312.htm (Accessed 04/13/2019)

[110] Eusebius, *Historia Eclesiástica*, Libro VI Chapter XXV.

Peter had such an influence over Mark that many, like Origen, referred to the Gospel of Mark as the Gospel of Peter. Apart from the possibility that the observation and mention of the young man in Mark's Gospel is the author speaking of himself in Mark 14:51-52, the Gospels make no direct mention of John Mark as an eyewitness of the life of Christ in a confirmed way.

This verse in Mark says: *"A certain young man, dressed only in a linen cloth, was following Jesus. They tried to arrest him, but he ran away naked, leaving the cloth behind..."* (Mark 14:51-52 GNT).

Once again, I cannot be dogmatic, but I would still like to present my conviction that this young man in Mark 14 is the same John Mark. Here, he, and the Apostle Peter with him are giving testimony about his presence at this event. It is not atypical that the author of a Biblical event might refer to himself in the third person, and on various occasions in the Scriptures, we can see this literary style of writing and expression.

We can begin with Moses and his expressions that, for me at times, end up being quite humorous. For example:

> (Exodus 2:2) *"Later, the woman became pregnant and gave birth to a son. She saw that he was a beautiful child and hid him for three months."* (ISV)

> (Numbers 12:3) *"(Now the man Moses was very meek, above all the men which were upon the face of the earth.)"* (JUB)

Another example is the Apostle John that uses this style, at least, five times in his Gospel:

(John 13:23) *"Now there was leaning on Jesus' bosom one of his disciples, whom Jesus loved."* (KJV)

(John 19:26) *"When Jesus, therefore, saw his mother, and the disciple standing by, whom he loved, he saith unto his mother, Woman, behold thy son!"* (AKJV)

(John 20:2) *"So she ran and came to Simon Peter and to the other disciple whom Jesus loved and said to them, "They have taken away the Lord from the tomb, and we do not know where they have put him!"* (LEB)

(John 21:7) *"Then I said to Peter, "It is the Lord!" At that, Simon Peter put on his tunic (for he was stripped to the waist) and jumped into the water and swam ashore."* (TLB)

(John 21:20-21) *"Turning his head, Peter noticed the disciple Jesus loved following right behind. When Peter noticed him, he asked Jesus, "Master, what's going to happen to him?"* (MSG)

Finally, we find, at least, one example of this style in the writings of the Apostol Paul:

(II Corinthians 12:1-5) *"Doubtless it is not profitable for me to boast. So, I will move on to visions and revelations of the Lord. I knew a man in Christ over fourteen years ago—whether in the body or out of the body I cannot tell, God knows—such a one was caught up to the third heaven. And I knew that such a man—whether in the body or out of the body I cannot tell, God knows— was caught up into paradise and heard inexpressible words not permitted for a man to say. Of such a person, I will boast. Yet of myself I will not boast, except in my weaknesses."* (MEV)

Nevertheless, if Mark is the physical son of Peter, just as all the married Apostles traveled with their families, it is normal that Mark, following his father, would have been present during several of Christ's teachings. These teachings became especially indelible with the relation that Mark had with Peter and the time that he would have spent with him. This, very well, could have included the night in which Christ was betrayed.

It is not difficult to believe that John Mark, the biological son of Simón Peter, was the young man in Mark 14:51-52. This is the reason that he is the only one that mentions the incident. He was there accompanying his father or had followed them from a distance because he wanted to be with him and like him.

## What We Know of Simon Peter

First, we know:

- That his father was named Jonah.[111]
- That he had a mother-in-law (Matthew 8:14) (Mark 1:30) (Luke 4:38).
- If he had a mother-in-law, it is undeniable that he had a wife just as we read in 1 Corinthians 9:5.

The three Synoptics mention Simon's mother-in-law: Matthew 8:14-15; Mark 1:30-31; Luke 4:38-39. Being that our principal focus is on Mark, I want to quote him. For, in this case, he was speaking of his grandmother.

> *Now Simon's mother-in-law was lying sick with a fever; and immediately they spoke to Jesus about her. And He came to her and raised her up, taking her by the hand, and the fever left her, and she waited on them.* (NASB)

Now then, we can learn several things from his mother-in-law from this verse:

(1) She could have been a native of Cyprus. However, if she was originally from the region of Galilee, she married an Orthodox Jew from Cyprus and moved to that island to

---

[111] The phrase "*Son of Jonah*" is one Word in Greek "Βαριωνᾶς", meaning, Barjonah. Matthew 16:17, John 1:42, John 21:15-17.

live her life with her Cypriot husband. It was there that her children were born.

(2) That she was the mother of, at least, two children. Her daughter was married to Simon, the son of Jonah. During the time that the Biblical record speaks of him, her son Joseph (Barnabas), was single.[112]

(3) That she was a woman that had come from a family of financial substance and material goods. How might we assume this? Her son, Joseph Barnabas sold a piece of property that was given to him as an inheritance, and he gave it to the church.

(4) That she, most likely, was a widow during the time of the Biblical registry. We can see in the book of Ruth 1:3-8, that a young widow had the opportunity to return to the house of her father. This was not the case for aged widows. For this, we have the first commandment with a promise, Exodus 20:12, *"Honor your father and your mother so that you will live a long time in the land that the Lord your God is going to give you..."* (NCV).

These widows lived under the care of their married adult children. The law of Moses gave the responsibility of the children to take care of their parents in their old age. In the New Testament, the Early Church took the care of the widows one more step forward. We can see this in Acts 6.

Given that, we can see the counsel of Apostle Paul about how to manage the care of the widows that were charges of the

---

[112] The context of 1 Corinthians 9:5-6, is that the words *"we have"* in both verses is a constant reference to Paul as well as Barnabas.

local church in 1 Timothy 5:3-16. In verse 16, we are given an instruction that would apply to our case at hand:

> *Let me remind you again that a widow's relatives must take care of her and not leave this to the church to do. Then the church can spend its money for the care of widows who are all alone and have nowhere else to turn;* (TLV).

The widows who are all alone and have nowhere else to turn were those that were the charge of the church.

In 1 Timothy 5:8, in this same context, the care of the widows, Paul said: *"But if someone doesn't provide for their own family, and especially for a member of their household, they have denied the faith. They are worse than those who have no faith..."* (CEB). Paul said that they were worse than unbelievers, because, even the pagans held the custom of caring for the widows and their families.

> (5) Now, if Peter had a mother-in-law, the next logical step is that he also had a wife. Just as any typical Jewish family of his day, it would not have been anything incredible for him to have had children. Why not, if in I Peter 5:13, Simon Peter said that John Mark was his son? Given this, I must ask, why is it so difficult for the Protestant church to believe and to concede that John Mark was, literally, the physical son of Peter, if not for the religious superstition that prohibits such a thought?

Someone could ask the question: *"But, Paul also called Timothy his son. Could Peter have used it to refer to him as a spiritual son just like Paul did?"* Yes, of course, and the question is a legitimate one. However, we know that Paul was speaking metaphorically because he was a recognized single man. Further still, Paul clearly said of Timothy that he was *"... my true son in the faith..."* (1 Timothy 1:2).

This is not Peter's case, because he is a married man and can, very joyfully have, and boast of a physical son. Therefore, we have no reason to make spiritual sonship our first, and obligatory go-to opinion. It is most natural and logical to conclude that if he said that it was his son, to believe that he had a son.

This mentality, once again, affirms the Catholic influence (with the idea that holy people do not get married or have children, and never have sexual relations with their spouses, because they are holy). Thus, many are not comfortable with the idea that Mark could literally be Peter's son. The Greek word employed in this verse is *"uihos"* (υἱός), and it means "son". Even though it has always been taken in the metaphorical sense, there is no linguistic or contextual reason to do so. The Word literally and simply means "son."

We also know that Peter was the owner of a house in Capernaum and that his mother-in-law lived with him. *"And Jesus, having come into the house of Peter, saw his mother-in-law having been put in bed, and being sick-with-fever,"* (Matthew 8:14 DLNT). It does not say, *"When Jesus, having come into the house of Peter's mother-in-law..."*

This means that Peter's house in Capernaum was of a Good size for its day and for the town in which he lived. It is also a good indication that Peter was a man whose trade provided sufficiently for the needs of his family and the support of his mother-in-law, that, as we have said, very possibly was a widow.

Fred H. Wight, in his book, *Manners and Customs of Bible Lands*, says of the houses of the region in the days of Christ:

> *If a house of two rooms is to be built, the Oriental does not place them side by side, as the Occidental builder would do. Rather the breadth of a room is left between the two rooms, and a wall is constructed between the ends, and as a result of this arrangement, the house has an open court. If the builder expects to have three rooms, then a room would be substituted for the wall at the end of the court, and there would be three rooms around a courtyard. If there are to be more than three rooms in the house, the additional rooms are added to those at the side, making the court of greater length.*[113]

With the evidence of Acts 12:12, it is very probable that the house where Peter went in Jerusalem, the house of Mary, the mother of John Mark, was of the family of Barnabas and Mary. This house was one of the properties that were the part of the inheritance left for Mary from her deceased father, who,

---

[113] Fred H. Wight, *Manners and Customs of Bible Lands*, Chicago, IL: Moody Press; Clean & Tight Contents edition. p. 35 1953.

apparently, was a wealthy man. Many Biblical scholars have come to this same conclusion.

For example, William Webster and William Francis Wilkinson, in their classical work, *The Greek Testament with Notes Grammatical and Exegetical; Volume 1*, says of Acts 12:12:

> *Mary must have had a house of impressive proportions to receive such a large group. And in agreement with this, we also read that her brother Barnabas (Colossians 4:10) was a person of substance (Acts 4:37). She also must have been a person distinguished for her faith and bravery to permit a meeting with such a threat of persecution over their heads.*[114]

The doctors Robert Jamieson, Andrew Robert Fausset, and David Brown in their commentary on Acts 12, reiterate this indication with almost the same words.[115]

Finally, I want to mention Marcus Dods, William Burt Pope, and Philip Schaff in their *"Popular Commentary of the New Testament."* They affirm:

> *We believe that Mary was the sister of the famous Barnabas of Cyprus…, who, during the first days of the existence of the church, sold a portion of his*

---

[114] William Webster; William Francis Wilkinson, *The Greek Testament with Notes Grammatical and Exegetical; Volume 1*, (1855) Charleston, South Carolina: Nabu Press, Reprinted 2015

[115] Robert Jamieson, Andrew Fausset, David Brown. Jamieson-Fausset-Brown Bible Commentary, Publisher Hartford, Scotland, Publication date 1878.

> *property and gave the proceeds to the Apostles (Acts 4:36-37), and that presented Paul to the Apostles in Jerusalem (Acts 9:27). This family, evidently, were of considerable economic and material wealth...*[116]

We see a particular case in the law of Moses in Numbers 27:1-7 that women, or the daughters of a family, could not be exempted from the distributions of inheritances. I do not believe that Barnabas sold the inheritance of his sister, but he sold that which his father gave to him. He was a single man and did what he wanted with his portion of the inheritance. However, his sister chose to use her portion of the inheritance, not only for her family but also for the work of the Lord.

Once again, we must think that these people were just like us with their families and every day cares.

Now, once again, I know that this part is speculative and hypothetical for us but let us consider what I am going to hypothesize for just a few moments.

## A Reality for Peter, and a Hypothetical Situation for Us

If as a faithful Believer, husband, and father of your family, they arrest you and throw you in to a horrible prison to execute you the following day because of your testimony as a follower of Christ, after having just executed a dear fellow-laborer, friend

---

[116] Marcus Dods, William Burt Pope, Philip Schaff. *A Popular Commentary on the New Testament*, Edinburgh, Scotland: T&T Clark, and New York: Charles Scribner's Sons. Published 1879-1890.

and one of the other leaders of your congregation a few short days before. What would you do? What would the brethren from your congregation do for your family if this happened?

At least it has been my experience, and I have seen innumerable times with others, that the brethren would be praying with my wife and family and caring for their needs, loving them supporting them and consoling them. They might even hold a prayer watch in your home praying all night for the move of the hand of God in your situation. Maybe they would do just like what we see that they were doing in Acts 12.

Peter knew this, so when he was miraculously delivered from the prison, he went directly to his house to be with his family, and to where he knew that some of the brethren from the church would be praying and ministering to his family. This should not seem strange to us.

However, it should seem tragically strange to us if, he was astoundingly liberated by an angel from certain death in the prison, was able to escape by just walking out and having the prison doors open by themselves until he got to the main gate, and just the slightest nudge opened it. Then he was able to walk home through the streets without being chased by men with swords and spears, but the first place that he went was to another woman's house to let her know that he was alive and well. That would just be wrong!

The reason that I say this is that, when he left the brethren in that house, he sent word to James and the other brethren, but nothing to his family (Acts 12:17). However, for me, it is logical that he did not send word to his family. That is because he was already at home with them! He did not expect to find the leaders at his house; he expected to find his family. Not having all the leaders together in one place was also the most logical thing to do under such dangerous circumstances. So, it was necessary to send word to them to let them know of the miraculous working of God's glorious hand!

Everybody was waiting for the imminent execution that Herod had planned for him. After Peter was delivered, going directly to his house was a completely normal reaction for a faithfully married and loving husband and father. We must consider that it does not explicitly say that he went to be with his family, simply because that is not the literary style that the author is using, and he expected this to be naturally understood.

Though Peter was focused on his family and personal life, the author of the book was focused on the event and the miraculous deliverance. His literary focus was not Peter's family. Nevertheless, for the reader of that day that was accustomed to the literary form of the book, it was taken for being understood that this was so.

Let me give you a brief example: In Acts 9:2-3:

> *In the meantime, Saul kept up his violent threats of murder against the followers of the Lord. He went to the High Priest and asked for letters of introduction to the synagogues in Damascus so that if he should find there any followers of the Way of the Lord, he would be able to arrest them, both men and women, and bring them back to Jerusalem. As Saul was coming near the city of*

> *Damascus, suddenly a light from the sky flashed around him.* (Acts 9:1-3 GNB)

We can assume that there are probably at least two to three weeks (and very possibly more) between the verses because of the time it took to travel that distance, and other logistical situations. This should be understood, but many times we must explain that today. In the time that it was written, it was automatically understood; no need to explain it.

Now my question is, "why is that we feel the need for the desvinculation of Peter from his marriage and family life? Could it be because of these influences that have been mentioned in the anterior chapters?

## Mark in Gethsemane

Mark is the only evangelist that mentions the young man that was following them in Gethsemane. It is in Mark 14:51-52. I believe that by relating this incident, the only thing that is added to the account is that the author is underscoring the fact that he has personal knowledge of the event. I know that we have seen this verse three times before during this study. However, now, I want to focus on the use of one word in particular and bring out an excellent point.

The verse says:

> *There was, however, a young man following along behind, clothed only in a linen nightshirt. When the mob tried to grab him, he escaped, though his*

*clothes were torn off in the process, so that he ran away completely naked.* (TLB).

*A young man was following along. All he had on was a bedsheet. Some of the men grabbed him but he got away, running off naked, leaving them holding the sheet.* (MSG)

*Now a certain young man had followed Him, having a linen cloth thrown around his naked body. And the young men seized him,* (EMTV)

It is thought-provoking that in the Greek the word young, or forms of the word young are used twice in this verse. There are very few English translations that use the word young twice. One of the few that I have found is the English Majority Text Version (EMTV).

The first time it is used in direct reference to the youth in the night garment, linen, or sheet.[117] The second time, it is used concerning the soldiers. Why?

This Greek word "young" is *"neaniskos"* (νεανίσκος) "youth". However, there are two applications and variations of this noun. This word comes from another Greek word *"neanias"* (νεανίας) which is between a child, and what we would associate with an adolescent;[118] for us, that would be a child of about thirteen years old. The second word is, "νεανισκοι" (*neaniskoi*), and the

---

[117] Strong's, G4616 "σινδών" (*sindōn*) A white cloth or garment -

[118] *Even though the concept of adolescence did not exist historically, until very recently. It did not exist in Biblical times.*

implication is a person older than adolescence, but younger than forty years.

In this verse, the first use of *"neaniskos"* implicates the sense of *"neanias"*; what we would consider an adolescent, but in Bible times, would be considered a young man. The second Greek Word used is the word "neaniskoi" (νεανισκοι). We would do well to make a slight difference in the implications given between the use of the word *"neaniskos,"* and the word *"neanias,"* when reading this verse. The term adolescent is in reference to the "young man" in the night garment. The "young men" "neaniskoi" that were soldiers is for the ones younger than forty, but older than childhood men.

This is why many translators do not use young men twice; because, in our day, one we would merely consider a child, and the other would be considered full-grown adults. There would be confusion.

### Peter's Sudden, but Temporary Dilemma

What we see here is a very young John Mark that has followed his father at a distance. Here, I know that this, once again, es speculation, but I believe that Mark tells us about the young man dressed in his night garment because it was an indication that he had been sent to bed. Afterward, he sneaked out of his house thinking that he was a man and wanted to be with the real men, not stuck at home with his mother and grandmother. However, things went very wrong that night and Mark stepped into a dire situation, and it nearly cost him dearly. The other much older, armed, and very dangerous "young men" grabbed Simon Peter's precious child.

Seeing this, shook Peter to his core. He did not see this coming, and it scared him to no end. All his bravado had suddenly evaporated in the heat of what he had just seen. He was willing to die for Christ, and even defend him with the sword, if necessary. What he had not considered was; was he ready to sacrifice his wife and child? Peter began to think that things had just gotten real! This was something that shook his sense of priorities and values. Everything was at the boiling point, and now his family was in danger because of his affiliation with Christ. What was he going to do?

### Back to the Garden

As per the identity of this young man, some scholars believe that it was the Apostle John (the youngest of the twelve), but John never mentions this incident. Others believe that it was James, Jesus' younger half-brother. Still, others think that it was just some random young neighbor that lived near-by that had gotten out of bed to see what the disturbance was.

However, many other scholars, such as Dr. Alexander MacLaren (1826-1910) in his work, *"Expositions of Holy Scripture: St. Mark,"*[119] and George Alexander Chadwick (1840-1923) in his work, *"The Gospel According to St. Mark"*,[120] also

---

[119] Alexander MacLaren, *Expositions of Holy Scripture: St. Mark*, Victoria, Australia: Trieste Publishing. 2018.

[120] George Alexander Chadwick, *The Gospel According to St. Mark (Classic Reprint)*, London: Forgotten Books, 2018.

believe as I do, that John Mark himself is this mysterious young man.

If this Gospel is, as it is believed by many to be, Peter's narration of the events, this would be another motive to mention his son in the Garden of Gethsemane. It also would be Peter explaining his sudden change of heart and his subsequent denial of Christ.

As we have said, all the Gospels have details that the others omit. However, the details of this Gospel manifest the evidence of an eyewitness account and can easily be identified as the testimony of the author. In a previous chapter, we spoke about the reason that Peter would have had such an influence over the life and writings of Mark. This is simply another indication of Peter's influence in this book.

## Following the Path of Logical Deduction

Logic is not a bad thing. Logical decisions guide the natural course of our lives. This, in no way automatically means that our decisions are carnal and far from the life and Spirit of God. The disciples lived their lives in love with the Lord, but that does not mean that they lived irrationally.

On the other hand, I am definitely not saying that God is limited to man's analytical capabilities. Because, when Paul wrote to the Corinthians that, "... *For the wisdom of this world is foolishness to God...*", (Iª Corinthians 3:19), he was speaking to the philosophers of this world that attempt to understand life without the God of the Bible. He was not talking about the common sense matters of life.

Speculation warning, but, if Peter would have had a son, would he not have been like John Mark? We understand that the Gospel of Mark is the narration of Peter to Mark, and you can feel that. However, this Gospel has also been written from the perspective of an active participator. You can also feel Mark's active participation in the events related in this testimony.

If Peter were literally Mark's father, this would help to explain how Mark became an eyewitness of many of the events in the life and ministry of our Lord. He was simply walking with his father, as his father followed Christ. Mark was a disciple of Jesus Christ even though he was not one of the twelve. Nevertheless, as the son of Simon Peter, he was a part of the larger group of disciples that followed Christ.

# CONCLUSION

I want to finalize this work with a summary of what I have presented in this monograph.

In the introduction, I spoke of the Egyptian death masks that now give evidence of an early first-century date for Mark's Gospel. The dates that they are placing on the original manuscript fragments are around the year 50 A.D. This date falls amply within the period in which a majority of the eyewitnesses of Jesus Christ would have still been alive. They would have clearly understood the context of all that was related, and how it was declared.

In chapter 1, I spoke of the importance of this Gospel, and that it served as the foundation of the writings of Matthew and Luke. I also presented the strong possibility that Peter was narrating his testimony, while Mark served as his writer. I brought out vital details about this Gospel, such as the evidence that it was written to Romans and their mentality. We concluded this chapter with some historical facts and brief details of the life of John Mark.

In chapter 2, I presented the Biblical plea of James 5:17, about the ordinary lives of the people that we find as our heroes in the Scriptures. I also brought out things that separate us from the environment and the culture of first-century Judea. The lack of understanding of these things can result in an eisegesis of the Scriptures, instead of exegesis. With a cosmovision and perspective influenced by an eisegetical standpoint, it is impossible to understand the drastic differences as well as the palpable similitude that we have with the lives of the people that walked with Jesus Christ with our present reality.

I presented the significant influences that have settled, in a general sense, in our mentalities. These things have become rooted in us because just about two thousand years of deviations and ideological interferences have come between us. These aberrations have come primarily from the Catholic Church. As a result, they have darkened our understanding and changed our concepts of the truth about the reality of the lives, and the situations of those that lived the original testimonies of the Gospel.

By seeing these historical events that resulted in influences and antibiblical decisions against marriage for the servants of God, we can perceive how a mentality has accommodated itself. This mentality makes it difficult to accept that these Biblical personalities had ordinary, everyday lives and families just like we do. They had simple and ordinary life situations, but this reality has been made incomprehensible for the church today.

These historical interferences make it difficult to imagine that the servants of God had families just like we do. They were husbands, parents, cousins, uncles, and aunts, and were also instruments that were used to do portentous works for our Lord. To think that they were people subject to the same passions as are we, just as James explained, is almost impossible for us.

For this reason, I presented the history of the introduction of the demand of celibacy for those that wanted to serve God. I presented, in documented form, how the Catholic Church affirmed that a married man is not able to administer the Eucharist. I also presented the Biblical argument in favor of marriage for all, and that to teach contrary is equivalent to teaching doctrines of demons according to 1 Timothy 4:1-3.

Still, the Protestant church, even after having rejected Catholic theology, continues under the influence of more than a millennium of indoctrination of this anti-biblical concept. Clearly, many struggle against these concepts more than others, but the influence persists in afflicting the Evangelical mindsets. Therefore, I explained that it is crucial to build an exegetical bridge. This bridge would connect us and help us to understand the historical, sociocultural, geopolitical, and philological environment of that day in the development of my argument.

In chapter 3, I spoke about marriage in the New Testament, and the reason for the discrepancies between the genealogies of Matthew and Luke. Seeing these genealogies, I spoke of the family of the Lord Jesus Christ, focusing on the lives of James and Jude.

In chapter 4, I spoke of Jesus' uncle and aunt, and the identities of Cleopas, Zebedee, Mary, and Salome. I entered into details about the cultural ambiance of Judea and the region of Galilee for the Jews of the first-century.

In chapter 5, I gave details of the life and relationships that John Mark had with other personalities of the Gospels and the book of Acts. In this chapter, I spoke mainly about Joseph of Cyprus and his relationship with John Mark.

Entering into chapter 6, I spoke about John Mark's mother and the background of her family. This discourse led us to chapter 7. Here, I developed the dynamics of the relationship that John Mark had with the Apostle Paul. I spoke about the severe case of culture shock that John Mark suffered, and the resulting care and discipleship that his loving uncle Joseph Barnabas gave him to restore him to the ministry.

This takes us to chapter 8. This chapter is built upon the exegetical foundation that I have been laying in the development of my argument throughout the book until this point. With this foundation in place, I present my argument concerning the family relationship between John Mark and Simon Peter.

With all this, I want to draw a correlation of the logical conclusions to which I have come with all that I have been presenting and what we have learned about these renowned Biblical personalities. First of all, we know that Barnabas was Mark's uncle. We also understand that Barnabas was the brother of Mary, the wife of Simon Peter.

Furthermore, we understand that Simon Peter was John Mark's father and that María was his mother. Therefore, Barnabas was Peter's brother-in-law. With this, I complete my presentation of Biblical evidence in favor of the biological paternity of Simon Peter to John Mark. I also affirm conclusively that Mary, John Mark's mother is Peter's wife.

May God the Father, Jesus Christ the Son, and the precious Holy Spirit be glorified and at all times and forever. May the Word of God be honored, read, understood, and loved. May the people of God be edified and motivated to love and serve the Lord efficaciously, and with wisdom.

# BIBLIOGRAPHY

- Andrews, Lancelot, *A Pattern of Catechistial Doctrine, and Other Minor Works*, Oxford, UK: Oxford University Press: John Henry Parker, (1847 – Public Domain).
- Agustín (Bishop of Hippo), *Celibacy and Nicolaísmo or Concubinage, History of the Catholic Church*. From Constantine to the Concil of Trent (313 - 1545).
- Barns, Albert. *Notes on the New Testament: Matthew and Mark*, Grand Rapids, MI: Baker Book House, 1954.
- Brown, Raymond E., *The Gospel According to John*. Vol. I. Madrid: Ediciones Cristiandad, 2000.
- Brown, Francis. Driver, Samuel Rolles. Briggs, Charles Augustus. *A Hebrew and English Lexicon of the Old Testament (Brown–Driver–Briggs 1906)*. Peabody, Massachusetts: Hendrickson Publishers, 1996.
- Bruce, F.F., *Commentary on the Book of the Acts.* (*Comentario del Libro de los Hechos*. Madrid: Libros Desafío, 2007.
- Bruce, F.F., *The New International Commentary on the New Testament*. Grand Rapids: Wm. B. Eerdmans Publishing Co., 1954.
- Bruce, F.F., *"The New Testament Documents: Are they Reliable?* Shoals, IN: Bottom of the Hill Publishing, 2013.

- Chadwick, George Alexander, *The Gospel According to St. Mark (Classic Reprint)*, London: Forgotten Books, 2018.
- Easton, M.G., *Easton's Bible Dictionary*, New York, London, Edinburg: T. Nelson and Sons, London, Edinburgh, 1894.
- Fabris, Rinaldo. *Paul: el apóstol de los gentiles*, (*The Apostle to the Gentiles*). Madrid: Ediciones San Paul, 1999.
- Gill, John. *Commentary on Colossians 4:10; The New John Gill Exposition of the Entire Bible.* 1748-1763, (1809; Dominion Público). Grand Rapids, MI: Baker Book House, 1980.
- Haile, Getatchew, *The Ethiopian Orthodox Church's Tradition on the Holy Cross.* Brill, Leiden, Netherlands, 2017.
- Hendriksen, William. *New Testament Commentary: Exposition of the Gospel According to Matthew.* Grand Rapids, MI: Baker Book House 49560
- Jamieson, Robert; Fausset, Andrew Robert; Brown, David. *Jamieson, Fausset and Brown Commentary*, Dominio Público, originally published in 1871.
- Long, George. "*Lex Papia Poppaea*", *A Dictionary of Greek and Roman Antiquities*: 691–692. Public Domain (John Murray, London, 1875)
- Losch, Richard R. *All the people in the Bible: An A-Z Guide to the Saints*, William B. Eerdsmans Publications, 2140 Oak Industrial Drive, N.E., Grand Rapids, Michigan, 49505.
- Lumby, J. R., *The Cambridge Bible for Schools and Colleges - the first commentary set published by Cambridge University Press.* Published 1882-1921 Public Domain.

- MacLaren, Alexander, *Expositions of Holy Scripture: St. Mark*, Victoria, Australia: Trieste Publishing. 2018
- Mitton, C. Leslie. *The Epistle of James*, Grand Rapids, MI: Eerdmans Press, 1966, p. 235.
- Mosterín, Jesús, *Los cristianos: Historia del pensamiento*, Madrid: Alianza Editorial, 28027 Madrid. España. 2010.
- Munro-Hay, Stuart C., *Aksum: An African Civilisation of Late Antiquity*, Edinburg, Scotland: Edinburgh University Press, 1991.
- Olson, Carl. *Celibacy and Religious Traditions.* Published to Oxford Scholarship Online: January 2008. http://www.oxfordscholarship.com/view/10.1093/acprof:oso/9780195306316.001.0001/acprof-9780195306316-chapter-11
- Schaff, Philip (1819-1893). *History of the Christian Church, vol. II: Ante-Nicene Christianity A.D. 100–325*, §33, pg. 256. Grand Rapids, MI: Christian Classics Ethereal Library, 1882.
- Treggiari, Susan, *"Roman Marriage: Iusti Coniuges from the Time of Cicero to the Time of Ulpian"*. (1993) Oxford and New York, Clarendon Press.
- Utley, Bob, *La Carta a los Romanos: El Evangelio Según Paul: Romanos*. Marshall, TX: Lecciones Bíblicas Internacional, 2012. (P. Cabral & G. Ramos, Eds., R. Gutierrez, Trad.) 2015.
- Utley, Bob, *The Gospel According to Peter: Mark and 1 & 2 Peter*, Marshall, TX: Lecciones Bíblicas Internacional, 2012.

- Webster, William; Wilkinson, William Francis. *The Greek Testament with Notes Grammatical and Exegetical; Volume 1*, (1855) Charleston, South Carolina: Nabu Press, 2015.
- Wight, Fred H., *Manners and Customs of Bible Lands*, Chicago, IL: Moody Press; Clean & Tight Contents edition, 1953.

# ONLINE BOOKS AND RESOURCES

- **Birmingham Theological Seminary**. Plummer, Robert L. *The Gospel According to Mark; Background.* http://es.btsfreeccm.org/local/lmp/lessons.php?lesson=GOS3text. 2200 Briarwood Way, Birmingham, AL 35243-2923. © 2012.
- **Clark, Laura**. *Papyrus Found in a Mummy Mask May Be the Oldest Known Copy of a Gospel*, Smithsonian.com, January 21, 2015. https://www.smithsonianmag.com/smart-news/papyrus-found-mummy-mask-may-be-oldest-known-copy-gospel-180953962/
- **Decker, Rod**, *Gospel of Mark/Latinisms in Mark's Gospel*, NT Resources, http://ntresources.com/blog/?p=1205
- **Enciclopedia Católica Online**. *Primer Concilio de Nicea*, Traducido por Juan Ramón Martínez Maurica. L H M. http://ec.aciprensa.com/wiki/Primer_Concilio_de_Nicea.
- **Latdict, Latin Diccionary & Grammar Resources**. *Latin definition for: consobrinus, consobrini.* http://latin-dictionary.net/definition/13407/consobrinus-consobrini.
- **Magister, Sandro**. *Eunucos por el Reino de los Cielos*. La disputa sobre el celibato. Noticias, análisis, documentos

sobre la Iglesia católica, a cargo de Sandro Magister, Roma. 28 de mayo de 2010. http://chiesa.espresso.repubblica.it/articolo/1343466ffae.html?sp=y

- **Merriam-Webster's Collegiate Dictionary**, 11th edition. April 23, 2008. Springfield, MA: Merriam-Webster, Inc.,
- Miller, David, *The Genealogies of Matthew, and Luke*. Apologetics Press, (2003) Montgomery, Alabama. https://apologeticspress.org/apcontent.aspx?category=6&article=932.
- **Piper, John**, *Barnabas: The Maker of a Great Leader*, Desiring God, Topic: New Testament Biblical Figures https://www.desiringgod.org/messages/barnabas-the-maker-of-a-great-leader?lang=es. 12, July 1987.
- **Slusser, Wayne**, *Gospel of Mark/Latinisms in Mark's Gospel*, NT Resources, http://ntresources.com/blog/?p=1205
- **Vincent, Marvin R**. *Vincent's Word Studies in the New Testament; Commentary on Colossians 4:10"*, Charles Schribner's Sons. New York, USA. 1887. https://www.studylight.org/commentaries/vnt/colossians-4.html.
- **Wallace, J. Warner**, *Is Mark's Gospel an Early Memoir of the Apostle Peter?* https://coldcasechristianity.com/writings/is-marks-gospel-an-early-memoir-of-the-apostle-peter/.
- **Whedon, Daniel**. *"Commentary on 1 Peter 5:4".* *"Whedon's Commentary on the Bible"*. https://www.studylight.org/commentaries/whe/1-peter-5.html.1874-1909.

# BIBLE TRANSLATIONS THAT WERE EMPLOYED IN THIS WORK

Supplied by Bible Gateway
https://www.biblegateway.com/

- **1599 Geneva Bible** (GNV) Geneva Bible, 1599 Edition. Published by Tolle Lege Press. All rights reserved. No part of this publication may be reproduced or transmitted in any form or by any means, electronic or mechanical, without written permission from the publisher, except in the case of brief quotations in articles, reviews, and broadcasts.
- **21st Century King James Version** (KJ21) Copyright © 1994 by Deuel Enterprises, Inc.
- **American Standard Version** (ASV) Public Domain
- **Amplified Bible** (AMP) Copyright © 2015 by The Lockman Foundation, La Habra, CA 90631. All rights reserved.
- **Amplified Bible, Classic Edition** (AMPC) Copyright © 1954, 1958, 1962, 1964, 1965, 1987 by The Lockman Foundation.
- **BRG Bible** (BRG) Blue Red and Gold Letter Edition™ Copyright © 2012 BRG Bible Ministries. Used by

Permission. All rights reserved. BRG Bible is a Registered Trademark in U.S. Patent and Trademark Office #4145648
- **Christian Standard Bible** (CSB) Copyright © 2017 by Holman Bible Publishers. Used by permission. Christian Standard Bible®, and CSB® are federally registered trademarks of Holman Bible Publishers, all rights reserved.
- **Common English Bible** (CEB) Copyright © 2011 by Common English Bible.
- **Complete Jewish Bible** (CJB) Copyright © 1998 by David H. Stern. All rights reserved.
- **Contemporary English Version** (CEV) Copyright © 1995 by American Bible Society
- **Darby Translation** (DARBY) Public Domain
- **Disciples' Literal New Testament** (DLNT) Disciples' Literal New Testament: Serving Modern Disciples by More Fully Reflecting the Writing Style of the Ancient Disciples, Copyright © 2011 Michael J. Magill. All Rights Reserved. Published by Reyma Publishing.
- **Douay-Rheims 1899 American Edition** (DRA) Public Domain
- **Douay-Rheims Bible** (DRB) © Copyright DRBO.org 2001-2019. All Rights Reserved.
- **Easy-to-Read Version** (ERV) Copyright © 2006 by Bible League International
- **Evangelical Heritage Version** (EHV) The Evangelical Heritage Version (EHV), New Testament & Psalms ©2017
- **English Majority Text Version** (EMTV) Copyright © 2009 By Paul W. Esposito.

*Bible Translations That Were Employed in This Work*

- **English Standard Version** (ESV) The Holy Bible, English Standard Version. ESV® Text Edition: 2016. Copyright © 2001 by Crossway Bibles, a publishing ministry of Good News Publishers.
- **English Standard Version Anglicised** (ESVUK) The Holy Bible, English Standard Version Copyright © 2001 by Crossway Bibles, a division of Good News Publishers.
- **Expanded Bible** (EXB) The Expanded Bible, Copyright © 2011 Thomas Nelson Inc. All rights reserved.
- **GOD'S WORD** Translation (GW) Copyright © 1995 by God's Word to the Nations. Used by permission of Baker Publishing Group
- **Greek Old Testament** (Greek OT), Deutsche Bibelgesellschaft, Balinger Straße 31A 70567 Stuttgart Germany. Revised ed. edition (9 Mar. 2007).
- **Holman Christian Standard Bible** (HCSB) Copyright © 1999, 2000, 2002, 2003, 2009 by Holman Bible Publishers, Nashville Tennessee. All rights reserved.
- **International Children's Bible** (ICB) The Holy Bible, International Children's Bible® Copyright© 1986, 1988, 1999, 2015 by Tommy Nelson™, a division of Thomas Nelson. Used by permission.
- **International Standard Version** (ISV) Copyright © 1995-2014 by ISV Foundation. ALL RIGHTS RESERVED INTERNATIONALLY. Used by permission of Davidson Press, LLC.
- **J.B. Phillips New Testament** (PHILLIPS) The New Testament in Modern English by J.B Phillips copyright ©

1960, 1972 J. B. Phillips. Administered by The Archbishops' Council of the Church of England. Used by Permission.
- **King James Version** (KJV) Public Domain
- **Authorized (King James) Version** (AKJV) KJV reproduced by permission of Cambridge University Press, the Crown's patentee in the UK.
- **Lexham English Bible** (LEB) 2012 by Logos Bible Software. Lexham is a registered trademark of Logos Bible Software
- **Living Bible** (TLB) The Living Bible copyright © 1971 by Tyndale House Foundation. Used by permission of Tyndale House Publishers Inc., Carol Stream, Illinois 60188. All rights reserved.
- **Modern English Version** (MEV) The Holy Bible, Modern English Version. Copyright © 2014 by Military Bible Association. Published and distributed by Charisma House.
- **Names of God Bible** (NOG) The Names of God Bible (without notes) © 2011 by Baker Publishing Group.
- **New American Bible** (Revised Edition) (NABRE) Scripture texts, prefaces, introductions, footnotes, and cross references used in this work are taken from the New American Bible, revised edition © 2010, 1991, 1986, 1970 Confraternity of Christian Doctrine, Inc., Washington, DC All Rights Reserved. No part of this work may be reproduced or transmitted in any form or by any means, electronic or mechanical, including photocopying, recording, or by any information storage and

retrieval system, without permission in writing from the copyright owner.
- **New Century Version** (NCV) The Holy Bible, New Century Version®. Copyright © 2005 by Thomas Nelson, Inc.
- **New English Translation** (NET) NET Bible® copyright ©1996-2006 by Biblical Studies Press, L.L.C. http://net-bible.com All rights reserved.
- **New International Reader's Version** (NIRV) Copyright © 1995, 1996, 1998, 2014 by Biblica, Inc.®. Used by permission. All rights reserved worldwide.
- **New International Version** (NIV) Holy Bible, New International Version®, NIV® Copyright ©1973, 1978, 1984, 2011 by Biblica, Inc.® Used by permission. All rights reserved worldwide.
- **New International Version** - UK (NIVUK) Holy Bible, New International Version® Anglicized, NIV® Copyright © 1979, 1984, 2011 by Biblica, Inc.® Used by permission. All rights reserved worldwide.
- **New King James Version** (NKJV) Scripture taken from the New King James Version®. Copyright © 1982 by Thomas Nelson. Used by permission. All rights reserved.
- **New Living Translation** (NLT) Holy Bible, New Living Translation, copyright © 1996, 2004, 2015 by Tyndale House Foundation. Used by permission of Tyndale House Publishers, Inc., Carol Stream, Illinois 60188. All rights reserved.
- **New Revised Standard Version** (NRSV) New Revised Standard Version Bible, copyright © 1989 the Division

of Christian Education of the National Council of the Churches of Christ in the United States of America. Used by permission. All rights reserved.

- **New Revised Standard Version, Anglicised** (NRSVA) New Revised Standard Version Bible: Anglicised Edition, copyright © 1989, 1995 the Division of Christian Education of the National Council of the Churches of Christ in the United States of America. Used by permission. All rights reserved.

- **New Revised Standard Version, Anglicised Catholic Edition** (NRSVACE) New Revised Standard Version Bible: Anglicised Catholic Edition, copyright © 1989, 1993, 1995 the Division of Christian Education of the National Council of the Churches of Christ in the United States of America. Used by permission. All rights reserved.

- **New Revised Standard Version Catholic Edition** (NRSVCE) New Revised Standard Version Bible: Catholic Edition, copyright © 1989, 1993 the Division of Christian Education of the National Council of the Churches of Christ in the United States of America. Used by permission. All rights reserved.

- **New Testament for Everyone** (NTE) Scripture quotations from The New Testament for Everyone are copyright © Nicholas Thomas Wright 2011.

- **Revised Standard Version** (RSV) Revised Standard Version of the Bible, copyright © 1946, 1952, and 1971 the Division of Christian Education of the National Council of the Churches of Christ in the United States of America. Used by permission. All rights reserved.

- **Tree of Life Version** (TLV) Tree of Life (TLV) Translation of the Bible. Copyright © 2015 by The Messianic Jewish Family Bible Society.
- **The Voice** (VOICE)The Voice Bible Copyright © 2012 Thomas Nelson, Inc. The Voice™ translation © 2012 Ecclesia Bible Society All rights reserved.
- **The Scriptures** (TS2009) Copyright © 1993-2015 by the Institute for Scripture Research (ISR) All Rights Reserved.
- **World English Bible** (WEB) by Public Domain. The name "World English Bible" is trademarked.
- **Worldwide English** (New Testament) (WE) © 1969, 1971, 1996, 1998 by SOON Educational Publications
- **Wycliffe Bible** (WYC) 2001 by Terence P. Noble.

CPSIA information can be obtained
at www.ICGtesting.com
Printed in the USA
FSHW010011100719
59842FS